Mapping Our Success
Periclean Scholars at Elon University

Creating and Sustaining Meaningful Global
Partnerships since 2003

Dedication

❖

To Eugene M. Lang whose vision and leadership gave rise to Project Pericles nationally and inspired what Project Pericles has become at Elon University.

Table of Contents

Acknowledgments

❖

The list of people who have made this program what it is today is long and diverse. Perhaps at the top of this list is Eugene M. Lang, whose original vision for Project Pericles as a national consortium ultimately gave rise to what we have here at Elon, and to President Dr. Leo M. Lambert for not only helping to bring Project Pericles to Elon University, but also for his unwavering support throughout the years as the program has evolved. At the Associate Provost level there have been two ceaselessly supportive administrators, from 2001-2012, Dr. Nancy Midgette and from 2013-present, Dr. Connie Ledoux Book. This program could not have progressed without spectacular staff support, most recently in the person of Ms. Catherine Parsons. We must include all of the Mentors who have given their time, talents and passion to the program and more specifically to their Classes. (Dr. Tom Arcaro, 2006; Dr. Jim Brown, 2007; Dr. Michael Frontani, 2008; Dr. Stephen Braye, 2009; Dr. Heidi Frontani, 2010; Dr. Crista Arangala, 2011; Dr. Martin Kamela, 2012; Dr. Brian Nienhaus, 2013; Dr. Ken Hassell. 2014; Dr. Bud Warner, 2015; Professor April Post, 2016; Dr. Carol Smith, 2017). Finally, this program is most grateful for the scores of people and organizations who have partnered with us in our various countries of focus around the world. Without their patience, flexibility, and vision, this program would not be the same.

Foreword

❖

What unfolds on the pages that follow is a road map for transformation and a remarkable story. One central idea, promoted by philanthropist and educator Eugene Lang, to call on noble people to change the course of the world for the better, would ultimately lead to the creation of a program that more than a decade later at Elon University has advanced the lives of so many.

To take an idea and make it an actuality requires the dedication and vision of key leadership. Dr. Tom Arcaro, Elon University professor of Sociology and an honored Carnegie professor of the year, has worked with dozens of faculty and hundreds of students over a decade to create a program that maps a course for sustained change. The centerpiece of the Elon Project Pericles program is the Periclean Scholars Program. Students selected as Periclean Scholars, working closely with a faculty mentor, co-enroll in a series of academic courses and select a project of global or local social change that they pursue in the sophomore, junior, and senior years. The inaugural Periclean Scholars in 2006, led by founding director Dr. Tom Arcaro, chose awareness of the spread of HIV/AIDS in Namibia, Africa, as their project. Arcaro and student scholars traveled to Namibia to do important work, raising consciousness about HIV/AIDS as a global pandemic and providing meaningful assistance to AIDS orphans in Namibia. This project had such a powerful influence on the university itself and faculty and students, that it changed fundamental understanding in our academic community of what can be accomplished when we combine the curriculum of the classroom with the curriculum of experience under the powerful mentoring of a committed faculty member.

Periclean Scholars have fostered sustained change around the world through intellectual contributions, advocacy, service and often pure grit. Working with faculty mentors, students have written successful grants to the Park Foundation and Pfizer to support their identified communities and mission, organized summits and global conversations, formed lasting relationships and in effect changed the world for the better.

The work of Elon University's Project Pericles program is a practical reflection of the name that inspired it, Pericles, the Greek statesman and change agent that brought to life the Golden Age of Athens and a body of work that would leave the world better than he found it. The same is true at Elon University. From the moment students are tapped to join the Periclean Scholar program, until the day we celebrate the milestones of sustained change they have created before their graduation, the Periclean program seeks to build within student scholars the hearts of active citizenship. We believe so strongly in this model, that in recent years we have turned our attention to assisting other universities, domestically and internationally, that seek the same powerful outcomes to adopt the model Dr. Arcaro and his team of colleagues have implemented with such success.

I encourage students to rely on this handbook as a fundamental guidepost to foster your own Periclean understanding and growth over the course of the next three years. We can assure you that the roadmap it reflects of Elon University's Project Pericles is a powerful journey of sustained and globally-influential learning that will change the course of your life.

- Dr. Connie Ledoux Book, Associate Provost for Academic Affairs

1. Introduction

Mapping Our Success

This handbook is a large step forward for the Periclean Scholars program at Elon University. By including a wide variety of information ranging from a record of successes by prior Classes to a clear and specific breakdown of the program, this handbook acts as a tool for both participants as well as for a wider audience of students, faculty and administrators, both at Elon University and at other institutions. This handbook will provide current Periclean Scholars will have a point of reference regarding timeline, standards, and expectations for their Periclean career. This handbook will prevent "reinventing the wheel" and create a medium for different Classes to showcase both their strategies and unique process of civic engagement and global outreach. In order to accurately depict the changing nature of Periclean Scholars, the handbook will stand as a living document that will continually be updated on a yearly basis. The descriptive nature of the handbook will be able to explain the goals, mission, and intention of Elon's Periclean Scholars in order to document the program and attract more participants.

Who We Are

The Periclean Scholars program at Elon University is part of Project Pericles, a national project dedicated to increasing civic engagement and social responsibility. We began in the fall of 2002 when the inaugural Class was recruited, and since then, there have been twelve cohorts inducted. We are dedicated to promoting awareness of global issues and to creating meaningful partnerships that can provide solutions to problems surrounding these issues in culturally sensitive and sustainable ways.

Students apply to become Periclean Scholars in the second semester of their first year at Elon. During the sophomore year, each Class of around 30 students chooses an issue in a target area to address. For the next two years, the Class engages in activities that integrate academic reading, research, and writing with service and outcome-oriented experiential learning activities. Many Periclean Scholars travel to their area of outreach. A Periclean Scholar's role is demanding, but makes a demonstrative difference in the lives of its partners worldwide and in the lives of individual scholars. Scholars have a wide spectrum of majors from over a dozen different disciplines, and they continually learn from each other and from those that they meet.

Our Mission

The overarching goal of our program is to respond in the most robust and meaningful way possible to the words in Elon's Mission Statement that reads in part, "We integrate learning across the disciplines and put knowledge into practice, thus preparing students to be global citizens and informed leaders motivated by concern for the common good."

The Periclean Scholars program represents a unique academic pathway that facilitates students - as members of a cohort - to do long-term and sustainable work on significant global issues - both social and environmental - typically in partnership with people and organizations on the ground in their country of focus. To emphasize: Pericleans never do service *for* our country of focus or our partners but rather service *with* these people and organizations. Our approach is described in the Periclean Pledge, a legacy of the Class of 2010:

We Pledge to...

Listen to our partnering communities, acknowledging they often have the best solutions to local problems

Learn about our partner communities' history and traditions, to better engage in culturally aware dialogue

Assist our partners in community-run development projects that will enable their long-term success

Responsibly study, document, and publicize our partner communities' needs and desires

Be **committed** to building lifelong sustainable partnerships, recognizing they take hard work and dedication

Embrace our lifelong journey of global citizenship through intellectual and personal growth

Being a Periclean

The process of deepening our understanding of what it means to be a Periclean Scholar is ongoing and demands constant and rigorous reflection and research.

We must always:

- Ceaselessly learn more about general global social issues and specifically about the issue(s) facing our countries of focus
- Probe more deeply into not only the symptoms of the problems generated by these issues, but the many root causes as well, that is, look not only at the *what* but squarely at the *why*

- Be educated about the latest research and news related to issues facing the country of focus and be able to communicate this information both academically and informally, in both word and writing
- Be informed about the actions and approaches of the people and organizations who are already addressing the issues facing your country of focus
- Act on addressing issues exclusively from a solid base of knowledge and fully informed of all consequences of our actions, both intended and unintended

The Program as it exists in the official Elon Course Catalog

Periclean Scholars
Director: Professor Arcaro

Periclean Scholars are part of Project Pericles, a national project dedicated to increasing civic engagement and social responsibility. They are dedicated to promoting awareness of global issues and to helping provide solutions to the problems surrounding these issues in culturally sensitive and sustainable ways. Students apply to become Periclean Scholars in the second semester of their first year. Each class of students chooses an issue to address during their sophomore year and then spends the next three years engaged in activities that integrate academic reading, research and writing with service and outcome-oriented experiential learning activities. All Periclean Scholars classes operate as seminars, with heavy emphasis on student ownership and leadership in most aspects of the class. Students from all majors are encouraged to apply. These classes are only open students accepted into the Periclean Scholars program.

Since the Class of 2010, all Periclean Scholars classes have counted towards a minor in the area of study relevant to the country of focus. For example, the Class of 2011, with a focus on Sri Lanka, had their courses count for Asia/Asia Pacific studies minor. The COR 455, which is offered Winter Term senior year for the Periclean Scholars, counts as an upper level capstone course. By becoming a Periclean Scholar and fulfilling a majority of the course load, (if you look below, 18 hours are offered for Periclean Scholars) you would be just two hours short of a minor in an area study. By becoming a Periclean Scholar, you nearly fulfill an academic minor and are able to fulfill a major Elon graduation requirement.

IDS 225 PERICLEAN SCHOLARS 4sh

In this foundational course, students develop a mission statement for the class and research in depth the issues and topics related to that mission. Emphasis is placed on becoming deeply familiar with the multiplicity of factors that surround the group's chosen issue and developing individual and group goals (short and long term). The class examines the process of learning to be effective and culturally sensitive agents of social change. Offered fall semester. Civilization or Society.

PER 272 SOPHOMORE PERICLEAN SCHOLARS 2sh.

In the second class of the program, scholars deepen their research on their chosen geographical location and their issue(s) of focus as they begin to put aspects of their mission statements into action. At this time, students will also begin to join forces and reach out to potential partners. As the class continues to learn how to work as a cohort, emphasis is placed on academic research, effective written and oral communication, and productive and sustainable partnering techniques. Offered spring semester.

PER 351, 352 JUNIOR PERICLEAN SCHOLARS 2sh/each

In the junior year, the Periclean Scholars cohort will continue broadening and deepening their knowledge of the content area(s) in the group's chosen geographic location and issue(s). The Mentor will guide and encourage the cohort to begin using the knowledge, conceptual

and theoretical frameworks, and skill sets that they are learning in their majors as they engage in activities outlined in their chosen mission statement. PER 351 is offered in fall semester; PER 352 is offered in spring semester.

PER 451, 452 SENIOR PERICLEAN SCHOLARS 2sh/each

These courses serve as capstones to the program. The students will put to use all that they have learned in both their earlier Periclean classes and in their majors to move forward their projects and goals. The Mentor will guide them in both reflecting on what they have accomplished and in planning for how they will begin their lifelong role as Periclean Scholar alumni, sustaining the initiatives they began as undergraduates.

COR 445 GLOBAL PARTNERSHIP THROUGH SERVICE 4sh

This course serves as a capstone experience for students in the Periclean Scholars program, focusing on development in a country or region that has been chosen prior to the course by the students. The goals of the course are to collaborate effectively in order to continue to learn about a variety of aspects about this country or region. These will include: politics, culture, history, language, social issues, and the country's relations within the larger world. Students in this class will continue to develop partnerships in the country or region of choice in order to work toward improvements on an issue affecting the people of this area. An overarching theme of this course is to require the students to demonstrate command of the theoretical and methodological tool sets that they have learned in prior courses, which include core courses, classes in their major, and all prior Periclean classes. They will learn to communicate their perspectives to their cohort, and effectively use these skills to meaningfully contribute to the various class projects and goals. Students will also be discussing issues related to grant writing, humanitarian aid, and sustainable program development. This course is writing intensive. Open to senior Periclean Scholars (or others with permission).

2. Who We Are and Where We've Been

❖

Description

Students apply to become a Periclean Scholar in the second semester of their first year at Elon. During the sophomore year, each Class of students chooses an issue in a target area to address. For the next two years, the Class engages in activities that integrate academic reading, research, and writing with service and outcome-oriented experiential learning activities. Many Periclean Scholars travel to their area of outreach.

A Periclean Scholar's role is demanding, but makes a demonstrative difference in the lives of their partners worldwide and in the lives of individual scholars. Scholars have a wide spectrum of majors from over a dozen different disciplines, and they continually learn from each other and from those they meet.

Mission Statement

Long Version

The Periclean program at Elon University strives to empower students through civic engagement both locally and globally with emphasis on cohort-based learning and student leadership. With guidance from a faculty Mentor, students work to create partnerships and develop a sustainable impact in their country of focus. The Periclean Program echoes the mission statement of Elon University and strives to "integrate learning across the disciplines and put knowledge into practice, thus preparing students to be global citizens and informed leaders motivated by concern for the common good." As Periclean Scholars, students challenge themselves through goal setting, both individually and for the cohort to explore the pathways for change.

Short Version

We believe in challenging what it means to make a difference
We develop relationships with global and local partners in order to create a sustainable impact
We are different because we partner "with" communities instead of creating "for" them
We believe that every student is a leader
And through this process, we just happen to change the world

History of Periclean Scholars

An initiative sponsored by the Eugene Lang Foundation in 2001, Project Pericles challenged ten colleges and universities to provide a learning experience that would "instill in students an abiding and active sense of social responsibility and civic concern." Elon University accepted the challenge, which fit with the university's stated mission to prepare students to be global citizens and informed leaders, and to foster an ethic of work and service.

Building on our strengths of student engagement and community service, we crafted an integrated program that invited students to become Periclean Scholars. The first-year objectives included the following:

- Foster a conversation in the community about ways in which Elon can better partner with local organizations

- Be more deliberate about embedding civic engagement and social responsibility in the curriculum
- Invite all constituencies of the university to integrate Periclean values into all dimensions of the institution
- Implement a systematic program for highly motivated students designed to enhance their awareness of civic responsibility and provide them with skills to be proactive members of society

One major commitment was to establish a Class of Periclean Scholars each year — students who are committed to civic engagement and social responsibility. All first year Elon students take a course called The Global Experience. Students completing The Global Experience provided a well-rounded pool of candidates for the Periclean Scholars program. These young men and women, chosen through a rigorous application process, take special courses their sophomore, junior, and senior years that center around a class project (chosen by the students) focused on civic responsibility and engagement. They acquire multiple sets of skills that empower them to raise important issues and solve problems in a complex global environment.

Students begin by surveying global issues, such as hunger in India, or AIDS in Africa. The sophomore year involves the selection and development of the project, which they see through completion in the

senior year. Projects must be creative, original, and most importantly, sustainable within the culture and group of people involved in it. Project Pericles not only provides an excellent opportunity to expose young men and women to social responsibility, but it  teaches them practical ways to get involved. As the program matures, each entering cohort is mentored by those who came before them and, when their turn comes, mentors the Classes behind them.

The first Class of Periclean Scholars, who graduated in 2006, adopted the mission to make both local and global communities aware of the issues surrounding the spread of HIV/AIDS in Namibia, Africa. Each subsequent class adopts their own unique mission.

A Note on the Naming of the Program

At Elon University, the program is called the Periclean Scholars program for obvious reasons; we are a founding Periclean institution and this program is a direct result of the challenge made by Mr. Lang back in 2001. There are 28 other member institutions of Project Pericles nationally, but our Periclean Scholars program is unique to Elon University. Other member colleges and universities have found other pathways to articulate their interpretation of the charge from Mr. Lang to enhance the level of civic engagement and social responsibility on their campuses. To be clear, though there are many institutions involved in Project Pericles, this is the only cohort-based, inter-disciplinary and multi-year program among all of the campuses.

Periclean Scholars as an Academic Program

Periclean Scholars is an academic program with service deeply woven into it. Each Class of roughly 30 students chooses one or more issues in their assigned nation or region to address during their sophomore year, and then spends the next two years engaged in activities that integrate academic reading, research, and writing with service and outcome-oriented experiential learning activities.

One strength of the program is that each Class acts as a multi-year interdisciplinary seminar where students learn to use and to communicate to non-experts the theoretical and methodological tool-sets that they are learning in their majors while at the same time learning about the tool sets from the majors of their classmates.

The academic courses that are taken as part of the program have been scrutinized and vetted by the University Curriculum Committee and are also up for regular review by outside accreditation entities with which Elon has an affiliation, most notably the Southern Association of Colleges and Schools. These courses include IDS 225, PER 271,

351, 352, 451, and 452 and also COR 455 during Winter Term senior year. As academic courses, each must include significant reading, research, and writing and, hence, have clear rubrics as to what is expected from the students. See Chapter 9 for sample syllabi.

A second strength of the program is that all Periclean Scholars Classes operate as seminars, with heavy emphasis on student ownership and leadership. The student ownership of the Class has typically included actively participating in the construction of course syllabi, with this role taking on more prominence as the Class progresses.

By the second and third year of the program, the Classes function so that each is broken up into various work groups with individual goals and benchmarks. In the first semester of Periclean, all students read, research and write from common materials most frequently assigned by their Mentor. By the junior and senior year, the reading, research and writing done by any individual student may be very different from her/his Classmates and there may be only one or two books and articles that everyone in the Class reads in common. The reading, research and writing done by each student is appropriate to her/his contribution to the Class and may frequently involve dimensions which bridge majors, perspectives and presentational formats.

The unique nature of Periclean Scholars, being a multi-year cohort based academic service learning program with diverse co-curricular and extracurricular components, creates challenges for establishing and communicating clear, consistent, and fair grading rubrics. Each Class and Mentor must face this challenge creatively and with a firm commitment to the highest academic standards. The expectation must be for each student in every Periclean Class to constantly be learning more about their country (or region) of focus and the issue(s) on which they have chosen to focus. The work for each Class and Mentor at the beginning of the semester is to determine the rubric or rubrics by which this work will be assessed.

With all of the above said, a third - and perhaps most important - strength of the program is that both students and Mentors are involved because they are honoring the fact that they have the high privilege of being Pericleans. The reward is ultimately intrinsic: we do what we do because we have a deep sense of social responsibility to, and feel connected with, our brothers and sisters around the world. We know in our hearts that to do anything less than our best is to sacrifice the gift of the positions we hold as faculty and students at Elon University and as Periclean Scholars.

Past and Present Classes

Class of 2006, Namibia, HIV/AIDS Awareness
Class of 2007, Honduras, Pediatric Malnutrition
Class of 2008, Mexico, Poverty and Education
Class of 2009, Zambia, Rural Development
Class of 2010, Ghana, Socioeconomic Development
Class of 2011, Sri Lanka, Environment and Education
Class of 2012, India, Empowering Adolescent Girls
Class of 2013, Mexico, Poverty and Health Issues
Class of 2014, Appalachia, Poverty and Environment
Class of 2015, Haiti, Restavek and Human Trafficking
Class of 2016, Honduras, Youth & Community Development
Class of 2017, Namibia, To be decided
Class of 2018, Zambia, To be decided
Class of 2019, Sri Lanka, To be decided

Brag Book of Past Classes

In the next several pages, you'll be able to see some of the accomplishments of past Classes. Please keep in mind as you read the following pages that most of the Classes continue to have an impact with their partners and their countries of focus through the Periclean Foundation. The Periclean Foundation is a legacy of the Classes of 2006, who began the predecessor of supporting partners with the Periclean Scholars Alumni Association, a legacy of the class of 2012. That is to say in true Periclean fashion, the impact of all classes continues to deepen and evolve.

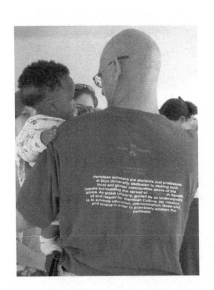

Namibia Class of 2006

The first Class of Periclean Scholars

As the inaugural Class of Periclean Scholars, the Class was always mindful that their actions and decisions would set the precedent for future Classes. As a result, the Class had two main goals: the sustainability of the Namibian partnerships and the program as a whole.

Media with a message

The Class received two major external grants making travel to Namibia possible for the filming of four documentaries related to the class mission of educating about the HIV/AIDS crisis in southern Africa. Two of the documentaries were official film festival selections, and all four were bought and distributed by Thomason Higher Education in their Introduction to Sociology and Introduction to Anthropology texts. The Peace Corps also used the series for training cohorts of volunteers serving in Namibia, and numerous university and high school classes have used them. Two music CDs were also produced as the result of this travel, and the sales of both the CDs and the DVDs of the documentaries were used to directly benefit the Class's partners in Namibia.

Bringing the world to Elon

The Class hosted four Pericleans-in-Residence from Namibia, three of whom founded their own non-governmental organizations related to the fight against HIV and AIDS. These Pericleans-in-Residence served not only as a resource for the class, but also for the surrounding community.
Such speaking engagements included speaking to high school classrooms and a radio interview broadcast nationally by NPR. The

fourth Periclean-in-Residence was a student from the University of Namibia who had attended the Class's Future Leaders Summit.

Partnering with the local community
The Class produced a narrative film that was based on a short story written by one of the Scholars. This film, centering on the stigma surrounding HIV and AIDS in the United States, was screened in downtown Burlington to a crowd of 500 and raised $5,000 to support a local non-profit, Alamance Cares, which deals with HIV issues in Alamance County.

Educating ourselves and others about HIV and AIDS
The Class organized and hosted the "Future Leader's Summit on HIV/AIDS," which was held during January 2006 in Windhoek, Namibia. This two-day event was a collaborative effort by the students, faculty, and staff of the University of Namibia, the Polytechnic of Namibia, and the Periclean Scholars Class of 2006. The event, opened by the Prime Minister of Namibia, was covered by CNN-International and was featured in a five-minute segment on Inside Africa.

The Mantra of Sustainability
Our Class founded the Periclean Scholars Alumni Association just before graduation. The Redwoods Group Foundation, made the challenge that the funds be matched each year by the alumni, generously endowed this organization. Their generous gift ensures that all Periclean partners will be sustained into the future.

Honduras Class of 2007

The Class raised $6,500 to fund the construction of a kitchen for the pediatric ward in the Mario Catarino Rivas Hospital in San Pedro Sula, Honduras. This is the largest public hospital in northern Honduras, serving more than 21,000 patients a month. The Honduran Office of Health and Nutrition estimates that 75 percent of children under age 5 are malnourished, exacerbating the immediate conditions for which children come to the hospital. Thus, attending to the nutrition requirements forms a critical element in treatment, and having a dedicated food preparation area enables these needs to be addressed directly. It also facilitates the provision of more meals per day, reducing the period between meals.

The class donated $1,250 to purchase school uniforms and bicycles so boys from Flor Azul, a rural community and farm for 80 abandoned and abused boys, could go to high school. Another $600 went to buy shoes for those who did not have them. The Class also painted a house, donated a half-ton of clothes, and held events to entertain children at Flor Azul and Nuevo Paraiso.

The Class traveled to Honduras in January 2007, and in addition to the service work that they did with the help of a generous grant from the Park Foundation, the Class produced a documentary about poverty and malnutrition in Honduras that was used by Elon faculty.

In October 2005, Karen Godt, co-founder and director of Help for Honduran Children, visited Elon as a Periclean-in-Residence. In addition to a public presentation to the university community, she visited with students in Global Studies courses to draw further attention to the plight of children in Honduras.

The Class created a **partnership with Hope for Honduran Children** that has been maintained since 2007, with multiple trips to Honduras being taken by members of the Class of 2007 in their postgraduate careers.

The outreach to Honduras by the Class has lead to the establishment of a **long-term relationship** between NGOs in Honduras and Elon

University's Kernodle Center for Service Learning. The Class has helped facilitate many Elon University service trips, as well as partnered with the Kernodle Center to sponsor Hunger and Homelessness Awareness Week.

Mexico Class of 2008

Dedicated to reducing the impact of poverty in Chiapas, Mexico through education, in partnership with Schools for Chiapas

The Class developed a deep and long term relationship with Schools for Chiapas, an organization that works closely with the Zapatista movement (EZLN) in southern Mexico.

The Class raised $15,000 for the renovation of a school in San Andres, Chiapas. These funds were presented to the governing Zapatista juntas based on the needs that the community members had expressed.

The Class produced a documentary about the Zapatista movement and the struggle of the indigenous people in Chiapas entitled "Painting Without Permission" that was subtitled in English and Spanish. The documentary was also screened at the International Step by Step Association (ISSA) Conference in Budapest, Hungary.

The Class organized and staged a successful awareness campaign, "Lifting the Fog," that featured video and photography of travel to Chiapas and Oventic.

The Class traveled to Oventic, Chiapas, the center of the Zapatista movement, in December 2006 and took part in the anniversary of the beginning of the Zapatista movement. During that trip, the Class painted a school with community members in Suytic, the home village of Comandanta Ramona. The Class also worked with the community to paint a mural with a leading Mexican Muralist.

The Class hosted Periclean-in-Residence Peter Brown, founder and director of Schools for Chiapas.

Zambia Class of 2009

Furthering development in rural Zambia through partnership with Habitat for Humanity

The Class hosted Periclean-in-Residence Lynn Twitchell. Twitchell has led Habitat for Humanity-International trips to Zambia for nearly a decade and began her own non-profit in the village of Kaoma. With grant money, a team from the Class traveled to Kaoma, Zambia in 2009 and filmed a short documentary about Habitat's work in Zambia.

The Class researched the ideas and ideals of Pericles and, in the end, contributed to the program what has been its guiding sentiment. This is from Pericles himself: "What you leave behind is not what is engraved in stone monuments, but what is woven into the lives of others."

The Class partnered with local artist Nicole Moore and raised nearly $15,000 for our work in Zambia through sale of reprints of her original paintings.

The class established the Take Action campaign to raise awareness about Zambia and funds for the Class's outreach.

The Class traveled to Kawama, Zambia in January 2009 and built two homes in Zambia. The team was featured on Zambian television for their work. The partnership with the people of Kawama deepened in May 2011 when the Class Mentor and another Elon team

traveled back to Kawama to build homes for two families with orphans and vulnerable children. This inaugural "Periclean Project" provided a template for future return visits to Periclean partnerships in countries of focus.

Ghana Class of 2010

The Class raised over $100,000 to support sustainable partnerships with Ghana's Volta region that...

Provide health services to 10,000 rural poor who previously did not have year round access to health care. The partnership led to the construction of the Kpoeta Community Clinic, medical staff housing, and drug store and staffing of the clinic with several Government of Ghana-paid staff. The facility is helping Ghana meet its Millennium Development Goals of reducing child mortality, maternal deaths, malaria, and HIV/AIDS. In 2011, the clinic was upgraded by Ghana's Ministry of Health to a Community Health Services Planning Center that can accept Ghana health insurance cards and is supplied with medicines by Ghana Health Services.

Support education in the villages of Sokode and Abor, on our own campus, and beyond. In Abor, the Class added over 500 Afro-centric books to the library of an elementary school. In Sokode, the funds raised are being used to build a kindergarten. The Class also gave supplies to Sokode schools and youth programs. Members of the Class hosted and gave talks on sustainable development in Africa, and published articles in scholarly magazines and academic journals. The Class's partnership with the U.S. Navy enabled thousands of books to be transported to Ghana free of charge.

Improve rural livelihoods via Heifer International and a solar cooker initiative. Dozens of families received bees, small edible mammals called grasscutters, and HIV/AIDS awareness training due to the support of the Class.

Promote cross-cultural exchange and lifelong learning. More than a dozen members of the Class studied in Ghana and nearly 75 percent of members who graduated are pursuing life paths related to their Periclean experiences.

Enhance the Periclean Program. The Class introduced a Periclean handbook, pledge, new lateral entry initiative, and a post-graduate common reading to improve student retention, learning, and sustainable partnerships.

Sri Lanka Class of 2011

The Class organized the Leaders in Environmental Advocacy Forum (LEAF) in Colombo, Sri Lanka in January 2011 and continued to discuss environmental issues by sponsoring environmental clubs at Panangala Mahabodhi School and Seetha Eliya School in Sri Lanka and Graham Middle School in North Carolina. Through these partnerships, an ongoing international social network was initiated which engages school children from both the United States and Sri Lanka in conversations about the environment. The documentary "The Elephant in the Room" focused on environmental issues in Sri Lanka and is currently available to stream on vimeo.com.

The Class expanded International Partnerships with the U.S. Embassy American Center and the Weeramantry Center for Peace Education and Research in Colombo. In addition, partner school initiatives included building a library at Panangala Junior School, Sri Lanka, creating an Adopt-a-Student program at Panangala Junior School, and starting a pen-pal program between Seetha Eliya School and Seawell Elementary School in Chapel Hill, NC.

The Class helped to continue involvement with Pan-Periclean Initiatives by initiating the Periclean newsletter, planning the 1st annual Periclean Scholars Loaves and Fishes 5K, and sponsoring two Periclean Scholars-in-Residence, Ajantha Perera and Chamindha Mahanayake.

India Class of 2012

Advocating for public health, locally and abroad

Through the Class's partnership with the Adolescent Girls Program (AGP) at the Comprehensive Rural Health Project (CRHP) in Maharastra, India, and their work locally with the Burlington Housing Authority, the Class sought to assist in the empowerment of others, particularly women. Thirteen members of the Class completed internships at CRHP, and the Class raised $10,000 for AGP in order to revamp a program on the brink of disappearance.

Four scholars, Brittany Moore, Katie Kenney, Sarah Naiman, and Annie Huth, wrote extensive research papers on subjects pertaining to the studies of the Class. Jack Dodson created a documentary about the issues affecting the Class's partners abroad. Six members of the Class attended the Clinton Global Initiative conference in Miami, and other members collaborated on a book by Edwin Toone. The Class hosted Pericleans-in-Residence twice, and met Khaled Hosseini and Edward Luce.

The class explored Lake Mackintosh and toured Elon's campus with young Burlington residents (affectionately known as Dream Girls), building cultural awareness and coordinating educational events for them locally. The Class encouraged dialogue with the Elon community with panel discussions on rural health care, and expended fundraising efforts to provide relief for those affected in Haiti by sponsoring a dance and raising $10,000 to donate to the Red Cross.

Mexico Class of 2013

We, the Class of 2013, have taken on a number of initiatives related to our focal area of Chiapas, Mexico, an area with a challenging political environment. As a part of Mexico with many indigenous Mayan, NAFTA has not only greatly impacted those still residing in Chiapas, but also those who have immigrated to the United States.

Our most significant project was the formation of a community support group, Hogares Sanos, for women in the Alamance County community with ties to Chiapas or greater Mexico. Beginning in July 2012, members of our class in collaboration with a public health graduate student, also a Periclean alumna, have conducted health

sessions on a weekly basis on Elon's campus. We arranged for transportation, food, and childcare for the participants and offered participatory "classes" with topics ranging from food sanitation practices to exercise strategies, based on the

women's requests. Through this project, all members of our class came to feel strongly integrated into the Alamance Community and tangentially to communities in Mexico through participants' connections. Seeing these sessions come full circle each Monday morning was very rewarding—as we realize our impact on a community that endures ethnic-based discrimination, living in fear due to rampant societal issues in Alamance County. It was amazing to see how a small group of us could change the feelings of this group of women as they put trust in us, and in each other.

Our experience with Hogares Sanos inspired us to record and publish the personal stories of our participants to shed light on the experiences of Mexican-Americans in our area. This idea stemmed from a connection our Mentor, Dr. Brian Nienhaus, had with an Alamance County woman who grew up in Burlington with her brother. Her brother had been deported to Mexico as a young man, previously never knowing a home outside of the United States. During Winter Term 2013, we traveled to his village to record his story, and the combination of accounts from brother and sister undoubtedly was one of the most powerful parts of the narrative we assembled as our culminating project. In spring 2013, we presented to first year global classes, accounting this story as well as the facts of immigration. In winter 2014, our Mentor's wife, Blanca Nienhaus, published *Aqui & Alla, Here & There*, which told this story quite beautifully. This Winter Term program, as well as our historical and written accounts, served as a powerful way for our Class to experience the culture and people with whom we have collaborated from afar in years past.

Today, Hogares Sanos lives on through the Periclean Scholars Class of 2016, who focus on Honduras, its participants, and our local partners.

Appalachia Class of 2014

Under the mentorship of Dr. Ken Hassell, the Class of 2014 worked to create projects of social change in Central Appalachia and raise the level of civic engagement and social responsibility at Elon University. They ventured to Appalachia at the start of summer, marking the start of the journey in their focus area. One of the recurring themes on this trip was the combination of rich land and poor people. Due to the exploitation of outsiders and corporations, the people who own the land are the poorest.

On May 20, the majority of the Class set off for Pennington Gap, Virginia. There, Sister Beth spoke with the Class about the history of the region and the relevant cultural issues that are still occurring today. From there, the Class went to St. Charles, Virginia, where they met Walter, Teresa, Ariel, Courtney, Bonnie, Rhonda, and Emily Webb – the family who runs the community center in St. Charles out of their own pockets.

After St. Charles, the Class drove to Whitesburg, Kentucky, home of Appalshop, a non-profit multi-disciplinary arts and education center in the heart of Appalachia. The Class spoke with Derek Mullins about what Appalshop does and what issues are affecting Whitesburg.

Next, the Class went to Whitesville, West Virginia, an area hit incredibly hard by the aftermath of coal mining. While staying there, the Class met with Lorelei Scarborough and Larry Gibson – two of the most active and influential figures in the fight against mountaintop removal. Before the Class departed, Lorelei expressed that she would like to purchase the building her center is in, as drug dealers live upstairs. Creating opportunities for younger children was also deemed essential; including health awareness, music programs and books All through the month of September, the Class partnered with Barnes and Noble for a book drive in the store in Alamance Crossing.

While simply leaving an area that seems so troubled may sound simple for an outsider, people remain due to heritage, family health, and an attachment to the land. The people strongly believe in the community and in themselves.

Haiti Class of 2015

The Class of 2015 is focused on ending restavek in Haiti and combatting human trafficking in the local community. Restavek refers to a culturally accepted form of child domestic servitude in Haiti where families that do not have the means to support their children send them away to distant relatives or neighbors, in hopes that the children will be provided with shelter, food, and education. Unfortunately, Restavek children frequently suffer emotional, physical, and sexual abuse.

Partnership with Restavek Freedom Foundation

The Class has partnered with RFF in Haiti, which serves children in Restavek through advocating for their freedom, educating communities, and mobilizing society to stand up for freedom. The Class is working to raise funds to create an endowment to support a girl in RFF's Transitional Home, which provides housing, rehabilitation, and preparation for the future for girls from severe situations of Restavek. This endowment of $100,000 would financially support one girl every year for many years to come.

Partnership with Alamance for Freedom

The Class has also formed a relationship with Alamance for Freedom, a local coalition in Alamance County that works with law enforcement, service providers, schools, and other stakeholders to address human trafficking on a local level. The Class of 2015 has established a program that will allow one Elon student per semester to intern for AFF, learning and disseminating information about human trafficking in Alamance County, developing resources for survivors, and working hand-in-hand with law enforcement for the sake of prevention and intervention.

Stand Up for Freedom: Restavek and Human Trafficking Education Week

The Class feels a strong responsibility to educate all members of the Elon community about the grave practice of human trafficking, and its elusive yet widespread prevalence and incidence on both global and local levels. In October of 2014, the Class held a week of events and activities in order to educate and empower the Elon community to end restavek and human trafficking. Five representatives from

32

Restavek Freedom Foundation, including the Executive Director, Board VP, and Director of the Transitional Home, were able to come to Elon for the week and bring an interactive exhibit about what it means to be in restavek. The week's events included a screening of *Not My Life*, a panel discussion with stakeholders working to combat human trafficking in Alamance County, a benefit concert at West End featuring student group performances, a speech from the director of RFF's Transitional Home, and student undergraduate research presentations.

Honduras Class of 2016

The Class of 2016 is focused on youth and community development in Honduras as a way to increase education, help foster positive health outcomes, and preemptively combat gang involvement.

Honduran Partnerships

Our Class has partnered with two NGOs that work within Honduras: Hope for Honduran Children (H4HC) and Summit in Honduras.

Hope for Honduran Children is a nonprofit organization that works with impoverished children in south central Honduras. H4HC focuses on providing a nurturing environment for children ravaged by conditions of extreme poverty. They do this through their operation of the Flor Azul Boys Community and the Casa Noble transition home. Flor Azul is a place where orphaned or extremely impoverished boys are provided food, clothing, shelter, and education, and

healthcare. Intended for recent adults, Casa Noble is a place designed to bridge the gap left by organizations that halt services when a child turns eighteen by providing job skills training and a supportive environment for these recent adults where each resident is carefully mentored towards a successful transition into adulthood.

Summit in Honduras is a nonprofit organization that works with rural mountain villages in the northwestern part of Honduras. They focus their efforts on medical outreach, education, literacy, clean water, and construction projects.

With these in-country partnerships, we hope to make a difference through focused projects that use our remaining time here at Elon efficiently. While designing projects, we are making a conscious effort to implement them in a way that is sustainable, the best use of our resources and time, and, most importantly, something that is requested by and valuable for the communities with which we work.

Local Partnerships

Our Class is currently developing a partnership with a group of Latina women who are a part of an organization called LUPE (Latinos Unidos Promoviendo la Esperanza). This group aims to promote community well being through organizing community building events, Spanish literacy classes for children, and public seminars on various topics. Members of our Class have become involved in helping LUPE with their Spanish literacy classes, and our Class hopes to expand this partnership in the next year and a half, depending on LUPE's needs.

Socially Responsible Business Summit

Our class is in the early stages of planning a multi-day summit for socially responsible businesses and social enterprises to be hosted on campus during the Fall 2015 semester. Over the past year and a half, we have come to understand the importance of social responsibility, as well as the effectiveness of social enterprises, and want to spread this knowledge to the rest of the campus. Currently,  we are compiling a list of contacts for potential attendees and outlining the goals of the summit.

Our Class is excited to see how our work with these partners, as well as the people of Honduras, will bring about lasting, sustainable, and positive change in Honduras, and how our projects with the people of Alamance County can help out here in our own backyard.

Our Accomplishments:

Since the beginning of the program, the students and alumni of the Periclean Scholars program have shared major contributions with the Elon community and in the partnering communities. Some of these other major activities include:

- Hosting over two dozen Pericleans-in-Residence on campus, most of whom are from or working in the country of focus of one or more Classes.
- Forging scores of lasting partnerships with non-governmental organizations, numerous villages and individuals, the US Embassies in Namibia, Sri Lanka, and India, and numerous schools and organizations in our local community.
- Successfully raising over $800,000 that has been ploughed back into our countries of focus.
- Organizing and co-hosting three major international conferences in Namibia, Sri Lanka, and India.
- Establishing the Periclean Scholar Alumni Association, now known as the Periclean Foundation, in 2006 to facilitate a sustainable commitment to our partners.
- The PSAA was endowed in 2008, thus ensuring that partnerships of all Classes can and will be sustained into the future, and the Periclean Foundation continues to raise funds and support partnerships created by alumni Classes.

Media products:

- Eight successful documentaries, five of which have made a significant, measurable impact far beyond the walls of our campus.
- Two narrative films, *Testing Positive* in 2006 and *A Rivers Reach* in 2009 relating to each Class' issues of focus.
- Scores of short videos available on YouTube.
- Two music CDs.

Some of our Community Partners Over the Years:

Class of 2006
- Catholic AIDS Action
- Lironga Erapu
- NENOWLA
- Ombetja Yhinga (Red Ribbon Campaign)
- The American Cultural Center in the US Embassy in Namibia
- The University of Namibia
- The Polytechnic of Namibia
- Peace Corps-Namibia
- The Bernard Nordcup Center in Windhoek
- The Putuvanga Middle School AIDS Awareness Club
- Alamance Cares

Class of 2007
- Hope for Honduran Children
- The Mario Catarino Rivas Hospital at San Pedro Sula in Honduras

Class of 2008
- Schools for Chiapas
- Zapatista Army of National Liberation or EZLN
- The community of Suytic
- The community of San Andres
- Redwoods Group Foundation

Class of 2009
- Habitat for Humanity-International-Zambia
- The community of Kawama
- The community of Kaoma
- Redwoods Group Foundation

Class of 2010
- Peace Corps- Ghana
- The government of Ghana
- The community of Kpoeta
- The community of Abor
- The community of Kpedze
- University of Cape Coast
- Heifer International

Class of 2011
- Rainforest Rescue in Sri Lanka
- The American Cultural Center in the US Embassy in Sri Lanka
- The University of Colombo
- Graham Middle School
- National Science Foundation- Sri Lanka
- Centre for the Environment and Development (Sri Lanka)
- Elon University Environmental Science Department
- North Carolina Sri Lanka Friends Association

Class of 2012
- Burlington Housing Authority
- The Comprehensive Rural Health Project in Jamkhed, India

Class of 2013
- Hogares Sanos
- Gradúate!
- Hillcrest Elementary School

Class of 2014
- Appalshop
- Barnes and Noble

Class of 2015
- Restavek Freedom Foundation
- Alamance for Freedom

Class of 2016
- LUPE
- Hope for Honduran Children

Pericleans-in-Residence Include:

Class of 2006
- Dr. Kevin Bales (author of Disposable People)
- Dr. Lucy Steinitz (co-founder of Catholic AIDS Action)
- Dr. Philippe Talavera (founder of Red Ribbon Campaign in Namibia)

- Matjiua Kauapirura (Polytechnic of Namibia student)
- Anita Isaacs (HIV+ activist and Founder of NENOWLA)

Class of 2007
- Karen Godt (founder of Hope for Honduran Children)

Class of 2008
- Peter Brown (founder of Schools for Chiapas)
- Erin Brown (Schools for Chiapas)

Class of 2009
- Lynne Twitchel (Habitat for Humanity volunteer)

Class of 2010
- Dr. Francis Amadahe (University of Cape Coast, Ghana)

Class of 2011
- Dr. Ajantha Perera (Waste management expert, Sri Lanka)
- Chamindha Mahanayakage (ecotourism guide, photographer, Sri Lanka)

Class of 2012
- Sankar and Divya Krishnan (co-founders of Tesseract Consulting, India)
- Edward Luce (author of In Spite of the Gods: The Rise of Modern India)
- Dr. Smisha Agarwal (senior staff at Comprehensive Rural Health Project, India)

Class of 2014
- Lorelei Scarbro - Director of the Boone-Raleigh Community Center and anti-mountaintop removal activist and Appalachian fiction writer who authored the highly celebrated novel *Strange As the Weather Has Been*, an intimate and complex look at life in Appalachia and the colonialism of mountaintop removal
- Ron Carson and Dr. Esther Ajarrapu the founders and sustainers of one of the most highly regarded black lung clinics in the world. They not only diagnose and help treat black lung, but advocate for victims of this life threatening disease in the courts.

- Bill Price, Resource Coordinator in Environmental Justice in central Appalachia for the Sierra Club

Class of 2015
- Adeline Bien-Aime (Director of Restavek Freedom Foundation's transitional home in Haiti)
- Christine Buchholz (Vice President of Restavek Freedom Foundation)

Class of 2016
- Karen Godt (founder of Hope for Honduran Children)

Sample Class Résumés

The following résumés are from the three classes currently enrolled at Elon. Each class is at a different stage in their journey in the Periclean program as evidenced below. Classes document their weekly progress and keep an ongoing résumé on the Periclean Blog. The function of this is two-fold; one to create a sense of accomplishment and visibility of Class progress, and secondly to allow younger Classes to learn from the Classes above them.

Periclean Scholars Class of 2017 Résumé

Mission Statement

We, the Periclean Scholars Class of 2017 at Elon University with a focus on Namibia, are still working on a class mission statement. As individuals, we are creating personal mission statements, but understand that even those, will be revisited and updated as we grow, both as individuals, and as a cohort. We have much to learn, much to do, and will put forth our best efforts.

Readings/Viewings:

Toxic Charity
Soul of a Citizen
Letters Left Unsent by "J"
Various Namibian Newspapers
- The Daily Namibian
- The Namibian Sun
- The Informante
- The Caprivi Vision

Discussion Forum and News Forum pertaining to articles from previous listed sources
A Measure of Our Humanity - Class of 2006
Various Documentaries on YouTube supplied by Carol

Class Activities

Created the class syllabus
For the "Good of the Group
Wrote blog posts
Discussion Board (Moodle) – Current Events
News Forum (Moodle) – Current Events
Created the elevator speech for the Celebrating Pericleans gathering
Group Projects/Presentation
- Culture
- Government/Politics/International Relations
- Infrastructure/Economy
- Education
- Health
- Geography/Environment

Information was put on Moodle documents
Conceptualized the framework for committees and roles in class
Created Committees
- Steering Committee
- Committee on Committees
- Fundraising and Grants
- Alumni Relations
- Media Communications and Marketing
- Events
- Social

Researched a few potential partners

- Hydroponics
- Community partner ideas from Duke

Discussion of possible project ideas in small groups in class
Created/designed a class t-shirt

Guest Speakers

Dr. Tom Arcaro: Director of Project Pericles
- Discussed the Periclean Program, the class of 2006 in Namibia, and allowed our class to ask questions about both of these things

Anita Isaacs: Namibian Partner of Project Pericles
- Q&A on previous Namibian class and on current issues and situation in Namibia

Jamie Smedsmo: Peace Corp Volunteer
- Shared her experience being part of the Peace Corps in Namibia and what she thought were important issues

Dr. Lucinda Adams: Faculty member of School of Communications, and member of the Lumen Scholar Committee

Sarah Vaughn: Student recipient of the Lumen Scholar prize
- Discussed what being a Lumen Scholar is, and the application process

Heidi Frontani: Class of 2010 Mentor, Geography Professor, Interim Director of AAAF Studies
- Discussed the experiences of her class
- Offered information and advice on the African/African American Studies program

Samantha White: Periclean Scholars Class of 2006
- Spoke to our class on what she is doing now and how Periclean has affected her decisions
- She talked about where she is now, what her experiences have been, and advice she had to give us.

Aisha Mitchell: Periclean Scholars Class of 2012 & Assistant Director of Corporate and Employee Relations for the College of Arts & Sciences
- Spoke on the progress and stages her class went through each year and offered us advice on how to -approach the semester
- Discussed her time as a Periclean and how it impacted her life path

Ronda Kosusko: Student Professional Development Center Career Specialist
- Administered MyPlan for assessment of our individual personality types/characteristics
- We divided into groups based on each letter
- Came up with qualities/things we needed from the class

Aiden Dyer, Drew Dimos, Caroline James, Kerrianne Durkin: 2016 Periclean Scholars
- Engaged in a discussion on how to strengthen the Mentor/mentee relationship and offered advice on how to continue our first year as Pericleans
- Asked them questions and they gave us some tips and ideas on how to run this class effectively.

Stephanie Carroll: Periclean Scholars Class of 2015
- One of the Student Advisory Group for 2017; offered advice on ways to approach our project and also answered any questions we had

Steve Mencarini: Director for the Center for Leadership
- Discussed various meanings of the word/action of "leader" and "leadership"; gave some of us a headache

Field Trip to the Challenge Course

- Team building and getting to know one another through different activities
- Posted in discussion board

Fundraising

- Periclean Cards- Raised $70.00

Pan-Periclean Activities

- Organization Fair
- Celebrating Periclean Scholars
- Restavek Week (Class of 2015)
- Freedom Foundation Benefit Concert
- Panel on Human Trafficking
- Poverty, Social Injustice, and Migration in Central America Panel (Class of 2016)
- Homecoming Tailgate

- Monthly Munchies
- Reading Day Open House
- Education of potential members about Periclean

Other Activities

- Discussion of possible project ideas in small groups in class
- "Good of the Group" discussions at the beginning of class, relating to possible partners, reactions, etc.
- Got to know other Pericleans through going to social events and getting meals together
- Conceptualized the framework for committees and roles in class

Goals for next semester

- Fundraising
- Begin planning various fundraising methods
- Global Citizenship
- Continue to discover what it means to be a global citizen
- Deepen understanding of Namibia
- Commit to attend 2 cultural events
- Continue to read/watch movies about Namibia
- Connections
- Get in touch with alumni
- Periclean Mindset
- Strengthen group unity
- Get to know classmates better (weekly lunches and coffee dates)
- Keep a "Periclean" mindset while abroad (i.e. don't forget about Periclean)
- Take risks and be open minded to all opportunities
- Begin planning Pan-Periclean Events
- Work on planning induction for the class of 2018
- Create personal as well as class mission statements
- Enhanced Knowledge
- Read Letters Left Unsent by the end of the spring
- Read Toxic Charity in its entirety
- Read more of Soul of a Citizen
- Read the blog more often
- Read more books that relate to community development

- Read articles weekly

Moving Forward

- Gain insight from citizens and professors on Namibia past and present
- Have a basis for a project
- Find more ideas for a class project
- Establish an area of focus for our class project
- Identify potential partners and contacts
- Based on both research and findings from our search for partners and contacts target an issue we would like to tackle
- Find organizations that are doing work in Namibia or would like to pursue it with us
- Reach out to potential contacts in Namibia and see if they have any potential projects we can assist with
- Build better relationships with potential charities
- Contacts/partners- It is really important to start to make contact with people in Namibia and North Carolina and learn about what organizations are already doing. Maybe from this we will be able to begin to pick a project based off of the work that potential partners are already doing.

Periclean Scholars Class of 2016 Résumé

Mission Statement

As the Periclean Scholars class of 2016 our mission is to make a positive, sustainable change in the Honduran community. As advocates for and partners with a Honduran community as well as continuing to participate in our field of focus, we will inspire others to become involved in creating positive change and strengthening the Periclean Scholars program for the future.

Partners

- Hogares Sanos – since fall 2013
- Hope for Honduran Children – since fall 2013

Research

- Reichman, Daniel R. *The Broken Village: Coffee, Migration, and Globalization in Honduras.* Ithaca: Cornell UP, 2011. Print.
- Levine, Peter. *We Are the Ones We Have Been Waiting For.* New York: Oxford UP, 2013. Print.
- Gelderloos, Peter. *Consensus: A New Handbook for Grassroots Political, Social and Environmental Groups.* Tucson: See Sharp Press, 2006. Print.
- Meyer, Peter J. "Honduras-U.S. Relations Report." 24 July, 2013. PDF file.
- "Honduras 2012 Human Rights Report. Country Reports on Human Rights Practices for 2012." 2012. PDF file.
- Donini, Antonio. "Humanitarianism, Perceptions, Power." *In the Eyes of Others.* Ed. Caroline Abu-Sada. US: MSF-USA, 2012. 183-92. Print.
- Gold, Janet N. "Daily Living and Lifestyles." *Culture and Customs of Honduras.* Westport: Greenwood Press, 2009. 69-77. Print.
- Leonard, Thomas M. "Honduras Today: The More Things Change, the More they Stay the Same." *The History of Honduras.* Santa Barbara: Greenwood Press, 2011. 163-76. Print.
- Pine, Adrienne. "Violence." *Working Hard, Drinking Hard: On Violence and Survival in Honduras.* Berkley and Los Angeles: University of California Press, 2008. 25-35. Print.
- Wolseth, Jon. "Contesting Neighborhood Space in Colonia Belén." *Jesus and the Gang: Youth Violence and Christianity in Urban Honduras.* Tucson: The University of Arizona Press, 2011. 27-49. Print.
- *Inside El Porvenir.* Dir. Erika Harzer. PS Film GmbH, 2011. DVD.

Speakers

- Barahona, Liliana, Melany Galeano, and Tesla Mellage. "¿Vos qué harás por Honduras?" Cargill. Elon University, NC, San Pedro Sula, Honduras. 18 Sept. 2013. Skype conversation.

- Godt, Karen. "Hope for Honduran Children." Hope for Honduran Children. Elon University, NC, Cleveland, OH. 28 Oct. 2013. Skype conversation.
- Levine, Peter. "Strategies for Civic Renewal." Turnage Foundation. Elon University, NC. 2 Oct. 2013. Workshop.
- Malburne-Wade, Meredith. "National and International Fellowship Opportunities." National and International Fellowships. Elon University, NC. 21 Oct. 2013. Presentation.
- Mejilla, Suyapa. "Honduran Cooking Class." Hogares Sanos. Elon University, NC. 11 Sept. 2013. Workshop.
- Springer, Jason. "MBTI Results." Academic Advising. Elon University, NC. 15 Nov. 2013. Presentation.
- Sutherland, Lauren. "Lumen Prize." Lumen Prize. Elon University, NC. 7 Oct. 2013. Presentation.
- Tennant, Shannon. "Periclean Scholars 2016 Library Research Guide." Elon University Library. Elon University, NC. 23 Sept. 2013. Presentation.

Class Projects

- Abate, Morgan. "Growing Up Motherless."
- Adams, Jennifer, Annie Goldberg, Erin Lanzotti and Bethany Stafford-Smith. "Honduran Food Fiesta."
- Bacher, Libby, Renna Durham, Christine Harris, Amanda Lazarus, Dawson Nicholson, Isabel Sackner-Bernstein, and Abby Senseney. "Cookies to Go-Go Fundraiser."
- Berk, Meredith, Christian Gilbert and Juliana Sierra. "Fall Fundraiser."
- Best, Charlotte. "Spring Induction Ceremony Planning."
- Brown, Arianna. "Raising Awareness about Honduras at the Speaker's Corner in 2014." ???
- Cianciara, Nicholas, Megan Griffin, Caley Mikesell and Erin Robertson. "Honduran University Outreach."
- Davitt, Liam, Anna De Dufour, Erin Luther, and Casey Morrison. "Hogares Sanos."
- Dimos, Drew. "Sticker for Periclean Class."
- Dyer, Aidan. "Reaching Consensus and Class Organization."
- Durkin, Kerianne. "2013 Honduran Presidential Elections."
- Fischer, Lauryl. "Establishing an Online Presence through Social Media."

- Harris, Sydney, Jenna Mason and Lexie Melanson. "Creating Awareness about Periclean through Multimedia Presentations."
- James, Caroline and Savannah Peery. "Gauging Students' Opinions on Foreign Aid."

Fundraising

- $322.37 through Cookies to Go-Go to support the class
- $103.25 through a Honduran dinner to support Hogares Sanos and the class
- $155 through discount cards to support the class

Media

- Class website. pericleans2016.weebly.com Created by Lauryl Fischer.
- "Cookies to Go-Go" video. http://www.youtube.com/watch?v=ipBOs_KGsgc#t=104. Edited by Isabel Sackner-Bernstein.
- "Education: A Human Right" video. By Nick Cianciara, Megan Griffin, Caley Mikesell and Erin Robertson.
- "Elevator Speech" video. http://www.youtube.com/watch?v=kggQFDq46NQ. Edited by Lauryl Fischer. Periclean Scholars General Information Prezi. http://prezi.com/aifqo1zrtnc1/periclean-scholars/?utm_campaign=share&utm_medium=copy Created by Sydney Harris, Jenna Mason and Lexie Melanson.
- Tumblr page. http://pericleanscholars.tumblr.com/ Created by Lauryl Fischer.
- Twitter feed. https://twitter.com/Pericleans2016 Created by Lauryl Fischer.

Accomplishments

- 12 of 34 students discussed applying for fellowships with Meredith Malburne-Wade, Associate Director of National and International Fellowships at Elon University.
- 6 of 34 students submitted an entry to the Human Rights and Social Justice Writing Competition at Elon University.

Periclean Scholars Class of 2015 Résumé

Mission Statement

We, the Periclean Scholars Class of 2015 at Elon University, strive to empower individuals and communities, in both North Carolina and Haiti, by providing opportunity and hope through the exchange of knowledge and resources. We will develop mutually beneficial partnerships, locally and internationally, in the hopes of promoting social justice and human dignity, focusing on the Haitian restavek community. While remaining conscious of cultural differences, we aim to raise awareness about modern day child slavery and human trafficking. In doing so, we aspire to encourage healthy and autonomous lifestyles for those affected by these issues.

Partners

Restavek Freedom Foundation (RFF), Burlington, NC
- Collaborate to establish a $100,000 endowment to support educational opportunities for girls in the Transitional Home.
- Hosted Executive Director Joan Conn, Board VP Christine Buchholz, Transitional Home Director Adeline Bien-Aime, Child Advocate Roslyn Phillips, and Exhibit Coordinator Natalie Hagan at Elon

Alamance for Freedom, Burlington, NC
- Establish an semester-long internship opportunity for Elon students
- Attend quarterly Coalition meetings

Events

Stand Up for Freedom: Human Trafficking and Restavek Education Week
- Facilitated documentary screening of *Not My Life* and discussion with Elon students
- Hosted local representatives for panel on human trafficking
- Alexis Keyworth, North Carolina Coalition Against Human Trafficking
- Jeremy Coleman, Burlington Police Department
- Rachel Parker, Anti-Human Trafficking Specialist from World Relief High Point

- Liz Leon, Program Director of Alamance for Freedom
- Meredith Edwards, Assistant District Attorney of Alamance County
- Produced a benefit concert with performances by acapella groups, Gospel Choir, & independent student artists
- Hosted a presentation by Adeline Bien-Aime, Director of RFF's transitional home in Haiti
- Showcased student research focused on human trafficking and modern slavery
- Collaborated with RFF to display "A Day in the Life of a Restavek" exhibit

Walk for Freedom
- Presented stories of trafficked children both in Haiti and the US to educate Elon students about the importance of the issue

Lecture given by representative from the Gray Haven Project
- Sponsored and supported representative from a human trafficking organization in Richmond, VA to educate Elon students about the issue domestically

Resurrection Dance Theater
- Sponsored performance of a Haitian dance organization made up of children who have come out of domestic servitude in Haiti in order to raise awareness on campus

Celebrating Periclean Scholars
- Organized speakers and food for a Pan-Periclean event

Periclean Induction for Class of 2016
- Organized induction event with speakers and food
- Served as mentors for the Class of 2016

Speakers Hosted

- Representatives from the Restavek Freedom Foundation
- Liz Leon: Alamance County for Freedom
- Representative from the Elon University Office for Advancement
- Elizabeth Conrad: Previous Peace Corps worker stationed in Haiti
- Jaimie Metellus: Elon student from Haiti
- Courtney Latta: Periclean alumna who has worked extensively in Haiti

Education

- Attended events through the Haiti Lab at Duke University
- Traveled to Mount Olive, NC: a Haitian community in western North Carolina
- Gave extensive presentations based on research on Haitian history/culture and current issues
- Read and discussed Haiti: After the Earthquake (Paul Farmer, 2011) and Little Princes (Connor Grennan, 2011)

Fundraising

- Organized off-campus benefit concert to raise approximately $300 dollars for the endowment
- Made, sold, and delivered grilled cheese in Monthly Munchies fundraiser events
- Collaborated with the Sport and Event Management department to organize an off-campus casino night as a fundraiser
- Raised over $250 to support a Haitian college student who serves as a translator in Haiti
- Sold Periclean discount cards
- Connected Elon students to fundraising efforts of girls in Restavek Freedom Foundation

Publications

- Maintain Periclean 2015 blog that regularly reports our progress
- Regularly contribute to the Periclean newsletter

Future Plans

- Continue to extensively fundraise for the endowment for the Restavek Freedom Foundation Transitional Home
- Publish white papers and news articles about the issues of human trafficking and restavek
- Write and submit grant proposals for funding the endowment
- Host speakers, show films, and/or organize campus-wide events to further educate students about human trafficking and restavek

- Write a newsletter for our supporters about our most recent work
- Update and add to the Class website
- Work with a Haitian organization to create graduation stoles for the Class

3. Getting started

❖

People to know

Directors

Dr. Tom Arcaro

Dr. Tom Arcaro is the founding director of Project Pericles and the Periclean Scholars program at Elon University. He was the Mentor for the inaugural Class in 2006 whose country of focus was Namibia. Dr. Arcaro has been a professor of sociology at Elon University since 1985 and continues to spread his wealth of knowledge to all that have the pleasure of meeting him.

Crista Arangala

Crista Arangala was the Associate Director of Periclean Scholars from 2011-2013 and has been working with the program since 2008. She was the Mentor to the Class of 2011, whose country of focus was Sri Lanka. Dr. Arangala has been a professor of mathematics since

2006 and continues to share her interests in inquiry learning both in and outside the classroom.

April Post

April Post is the current Associate Director of Periclean Scholars serving from 2014-present. She is currently the Mentor of the Class of 2016, whose country of focus is Honduras.

Mentors

Dr. Tom Arcaro (arcaro@elon.edu) Department of Sociology and Anthropology, Class of 2006 (HIV/AIDS awareness/education in Namibia)

Dr. Jim Brown (brownjim@elon.edu) Department of History and Geography, Class of 2007 (Reducing malnutrition in Honduras)

Dr. Michael Frontani (mfrontani@elon.edu) Communications Department, Class of 2008 (Cultural survival and access to education for Mayans in Chiapas, Mexico)

Dr. Stephen Braye (brayes@elon.edu) Department of English, Class of 2009 (Providing housing for Angolan refugees in Zambia through Habitat for Humanity International)

Dr. Heidi Frontani (glaesel@elon.edu) Department of History and Geography, Class of 2010 (Improving access to healthcare, increasing food security, and providing educational materials in three communities in Ghana's Volta Region)

Dr. Crista Arangala (ccoles@elon.edu) Department of Mathematics, Class of 2011 (Environmental conservation and education efforts in Sri Lanka)

Dr. Martin Kamela (mkamela@elon.edu) Department of Physics, Class of 2012 (Empowering adolescent girls in Jamkhed, India)

Dr. Brian Nienhaus (bnienhaus@elon.edu) Department of Business, Class of 2013 (Working on issues of education and healthcare in Chiapas)

Dr. Ken Hassell (hassell@elon.edu) Department of Art, Class of 2014 (Mountaintop removal in Appalachia)

Dr. Bud Warner (bwarner3@elon.edu) Department of Human Service Studies, Class of 2015 (Restavek and Human Trafficking in Haiti)

April Post (apost@elon.edu) Department of Foreign Languages and Cultures, Class of 2016 (Community and Youth Development in Honduras)

Dr. Carol Smith (csmith@elon.edu) Department of Health and Human Performance, Class of 2017 (Namibia concentration)

Dr. Steve Braye (brayes@elon.edu) Department of English, Class of 2018 (Zambia concentration)

Dr. Matt Gendel (mgendel@elon.edu) Department of Psychology, Class of 2019 (Sri Lanka concentration)

Note: The range of departments and schools represented by the Mentors above is reflective of the range of majors represented by the students who become Periclean Scholars. This is by design and we believe that it is one strength of the program.

Means of Communication

Moodle

Moodle is an efficient means of communication for Periclean Scholars Class. There will be a Moodle account for every individual Periclean Scholars Class as well as a general Pan-Periclean Scholars account. Some important features include the ability to email the Class under the 'Quick Mail' section, by selecting 'Compose New Mail.' If your Class forms different topic and interest groups then you can also email each group separately. The Moodle discussion page allows different discussion boards to be created where all Class members can post questions and important thoughts on project partnerships, fundraising ideas, and reading discussions. Moodle is also a useful place to post important documents, such as the Pericleans-in-Residence schedule, readings, schedules for meal-swipe Moseley table times, three-year plans, and grant proposals.

E-net

E-net is an electronic news center for the Elon University Community. Under E-Net you can post information on upcoming events, available jobs, volunteer opportunities, and other general news on Elon's website. In order to approve your E-net request, you must submit your request a day before you would like it to appear.

Pendulum

The Pendulum is Elon's weekly printed and online newspaper. It has been very helpful in supporting Periclean events and milestones. Informing them a week ahead of any events would allow them to have someone at the event. However, having someone contact one of the editors a few weeks in advance could help in promoting the event, making higher attendance possible.

Table Tents

These are the tri-folds found on tables in common eating areas on campus. They can be used to advertise events and applying for Periclean Scholars. The form can be found on the Dining Services website: http://www.campusdish.com/en-US/CSSE/Elon/NewsEvents/OnlineForms.htmf

Moseley Digital Boards

Forms and directions can be found on the Moseley Website:
http://www.elon.edu/e-web/students/campuscenter/fund.xhtml

Facebook

Several Classes have used Facebook to create a group for their Class.
They have also advertised events and fundraisers.

Webpage

Call the Technology Help Desk at x5200 to create an account for a
webpage for your Class. No actual webpage will exist unless the
Mentor or one of the Pericleans in that Class creates the website, using a web design program and then publishing it to the Internet. Your webpage account will have the following name: http://org.elon.edu/pericleanscholarsXXXX (the XXXX would contain the year of your particular Class).

A Periclean, Faculty Mentor, or third party can maintain the page, but he/she will need to have familiarity with webpage design. If you want the page to be updated after your Class graduates, keep this in mind when designating your Webmaster.

If, as the Mentor, you will be maintaining your Periclean Scholars webpage and you want it to have a more professional look, you may want to look into getting Adobe Create Suite III (around $250) or other web design program installed on your computer.

Your website can be an effective approach to letting a lot of people know about your projects and how they can help. Consider adding a link to your website onto your signature file in your email. Consider encouraging your Pericleans to do the same with their signature files.

4. Being a Periclean Scholar

❖

Being a Periclean Scholar at Elon University is a privilege and an honor. It is a multi-year commitment at the undergraduate level that can become a lifetime commitment after graduation. Being involved as a Periclean Scholar is a demanding role, but one that makes a demonstrative difference not only in the lives of the individual Periclean Scholars, but in the lives of the many partners we have world wide. Below is a year-by-year description of what being a Periclean Scholar involves.

Year 0 (first year at Elon)

- Work on team building with your Class at, and after, the Induction Ceremony
- Identify other Pericleans in your Class who may share your major, interests, and/or skill sets and begin to imagine how you can team together on various group initiatives that might move you and your Class forward toward your goals
- Stay in touch and keep networking and team building during the summer (remember, social justice and environmental issues do not function on an academic calendar)

Note: the following lists are for the most part cumulative, and what goes for one year goes for the others. Consider this a guide or break down of personal responsibilities for each year of involvement in the program.

Year 1 (sophomore year)

Course: IDS 225 Periclean Scholars

In this foundational course, students develop a mission statement for the class and complete in depth research about the issues and topics related to that mission. Emphasis is placed on becoming deeply familiar with the multiplicity of factors that surround the group's chosen issue as well as developing individual and group goals, both short and long term.

Responsibilities:

- Be involved in non-Periclean activities, but always make being a Periclean Scholar one of your very top priorities
- Attend every Periclean class and do more homework than you are assigned, learning as much as you can about your country/region of focus
- Begin working on your individual three-year plan, making sure to incorporate your major and any Fellows (Honors, Leadership, Communications, Business, Teaching, Elon College, etc.) projects into this plan as much as possible
- Contribute meaningfully in the design of your Class three year plan
- Each Class needs to decide how to decide, i.e., how decisions will be made about focus, fundraising, travel, etc. Be a part of this discussion

- Help your Class to identify and vet (and be willing to be vetted by) partners both locally and in your country/region of focus
- Begin thinking about who you may want to invite to campus as a Periclean in Residence.
- Keep in close contact with your academic advisor, making sure to count your Periclean hours appropriately to your major and minor(s). In most cases, Periclean Scholars will be able to count their PER hours toward a minor (e.g., the 2011's and 2012's can count their hours toward a minor in Asia/Asian Pacific Studies minor)
- With your academic advisor work out your study abroad plans for your Elon career, keeping in mind that it is likely that your Class may choose to travel to their country/region of focus winter term senior year. This travel, as are all Elon study abroad experiences, is student funded, and you will need to plan for this financial burden
- Consider applying for a Lumen Prize and/or SURE research that you can relate to your Class mission and goals
- Plan Induction Ceremony for incoming Periclean scholars

Courses: PER 272 Sophomore Periclean Scholars

In the second semester of sophomore year, the Periclean Scholars continue working as a class to brainstorm potential partners and projects as well as working to establish goals for the future. As this course meets only once a week, emphasis is placed on group work outside of class time where students can further their knowledge of their area of focus and establish connections wherever they may apply.

Year 2 (junior year)

Courses: PER 351/352 Junior Periclean Scholars

In the junior year, the Periclean Scholars continue broadening and deepening their knowledge of the content area(s) in the group's chosen geographic location and/or issue(s). The Mentor (Professor) will guide and encourage the cohort to begin using the knowledge, conceptual and theoretical frameworks, and skill sets that they are learning in their academic majors as they engage in activities outlined in their chosen mission statement.

Responsibilities:

- Again, be involved in non-Periclean activities, but always make being a Periclean Scholar one of your very top priorities
- During junior year many Pericleans spend a semester abroad. It is likely that both fall and spring semester you will "lose" as many as 7-8 of your classmates, often key players in terms of team dynamics. Class morale and team building may take special effort
- Work with your Class to revisit your Class mission statement and three-year plan
- In second semester, identify classmates to be nominated for Periclean Scholar of the Year (goes to rising senior)
- Consider presenting research that you have done related to Periclean in SURF and/or NCUR
- If your Class is planning a senior winter term travel to your country/region of focus begin your planning now. Fall can be used for brainstorming, but by mid spring you need to begin committing to a plan
- Plan Celebrating Periclean (See Pan-Periclean chapter: Celebrating Periclean)

Year 3 (senior year)

Courses: PER 451/452 Senior Periclean Scholars, COR 455 Global Partnership Through Service

These courses serve as a capstone to the program. The students fully implement all that they have learned in both their earlier Periclean classes as well as their academic majors in order to address the projects and goals that they set out to complete from the beginning of their experience.

Responsibilities:

- In the fall, if your Class has designed a capstone project in your country/region of focus, you will need to take an active part in this planning
- Always be thinking of a way that your class assignments in any of your classes can be used to benefit your Periclean Scholar Class (e.g., if you have a class in digital media convergence do a project highlighting your Class initiatives)
- Always be thinking of how you can focus your capstone assignments for your Fellows involvement into Periclean (e.g., Emily Sears and Hayley Gravette, '06, dedicated their "common good" project to organizing the event where Testing Positive was screened as a fundraiser)
- Always be thinking of how you can focus your senior seminar (for your major) efforts into work related to your Class efforts
- Plan for end-of-year events such as the senior banquet. Get prepared for the end of this chapter of being a Periclean Scholar
- Plan for sustainability of your efforts beyond graduation. This includes representation on the Periclean Foundation Steering Committee and stewardship of the various initiatives and partnerships that you began in the last three years

Years 4+ (post graduation)

- Upon graduation you become a member of the Periclean Foundation
- Consider taking on a two tier term being your Class representative on the Steering Committee of the Periclean Foundation
- Stay in communication with your Classmates and your Mentor using all appropriate social networking vehicles; make sure that your Mentor and the Director have your contact information (email, mailing address, employment/graduate school, etc. status)
- Donate regularly to Elon University and designate your gift to go directly to Project Pericles knowing that these funds will

go directly to the Periclean Foundation and will directly benefit the partners that Classes vetted

- Find out if the organization or business that you work in has a philanthropic outreach office and find out how this entity might be a resource for the Periclean Foundation
- Find out if the organization or business that you work for has a matching program for donations
- Continue to research and keep up with your country/region of focus and the issues that drove your class
- Continue to maintain contact with the organizations with which your Class partnered, and especially the individuals that your Class invited to campus as Pericleans-in-Residence
- Keep in communication with the Elon University Alumni Relations office and be aware of travel opportunities back to your country/region of focus
- Consider writing a short article for the newsletter about your life and career especially as they have been impacted by your undergraduate experience as a Periclean Scholar
- Always remember the reason you made the commitment to become a Periclean Scholar as a first-year student at Elon. Never ever let that passion wane because it is you at your best and, more importantly, you continue to make a difference in our world as a true global citizen

Continual Efforts and Key Points:

Use the statements below as a general checklist in ensuring yourself accountable as a Periclean Scholar

- Be involved in non-Periclean activities, but always make being a Periclean Scholar one of your very top priorities
- Attend every Periclean class and do more homework than you are assigned
- Be willing to put in extra time outside of the scheduled classes and meetings for research, networking, attending related speakers, exploring and planning fundraising opportunities, etc.
- If you go abroad, stay current with your Class by remaining active via Moodle, email and other social media avenues. While abroad seek out ways to move forward the vision of your Class via contacts in your country of study (e.g., the

2013's who studied abroad found groups knowledgeable about the politics of Chiapas in nearly any major city around the world, and so on)

- Work on team building with your Class both during formal class time and also beyond class time socially. This means communicating effectively and building a rock solid base of trust and mutual respect
- Work on your relationship with your Mentor
- Attend Pan-Periclean events and events planned by the other Classes, especially events featuring Pericleans-in-Residence
- Always have your "elevator speech" updated and polished so that you can take advantage of those moments to tell others about the program keeping in mind that every time you talk about Periclean you are advancing the goal of engendering global awareness and civic engagement

Director's Reflection

As Director, I [Dr. Tom Arcaro] have devoted a good deal of my research and writing energies in the last decade to learning more about what it means to be a global citizen and to act on knowledge about global social issues. Our program is, in one sense, a multi-pronged NGO doing both aid and development work around the world. As each Class begins to partner with people and organizations dealing with the issues in their country, they have the serious responsibility to vet - and be vetted by - these people and organizations. This vetting process must ask the hard questions, examining factors such as the messages in their mission statement, overall transparency of operations, sustainability plans and practices, and, critically, the cultural sensitivity and thoughtfulness with which any aid or development work is done. This vetting involves constant research that must remain a central focus of any Class.

At bare minimum, each Periclean and her/his Class must clearly understand that there is a tremendous difference between "giving" and "partnering." Giving to a cause, for example donating cans of soup to the local shelter or sending a check to aid the hungry in Honduras, represents a meaningful act. At times, this can be better than not doing those acts of charity. Overall though, partnering is

more; more meaningful, more difficult, and more time consuming.
Here is a summary of the differences and similarities:

Giving vs. Partnering

	"Giving"	"Partnering"
Fast?	Yes	No
Easy?	Yes	No
Pathway to sustainability?	No	Strong possibility.
Involve teamwork?	Not typically	Virtually always
Helpful to your partners?	Sometimes yes, with many, many qualifications	Yes, with qualifications
Is there a meaningful connection?	No. In some cases, just the opposite.	Yes, if done right
Culturally sensitive?	Frequently not	Done right, yes
The Periclean way	No	Yes

Doing bad by doing good

The literature on the history and nature of humanitarian aid and
development work is growing rapidly, much like the field itself. There
continues to be a robust - though largely unresolved - discussion of
how best to proceed with aid. The Jeffery Sachs (*The End of Poverty*)
versus William Easterly (*White Man's Burden*) tug of war is
instructive, and a close read of their works leaves one better informed
but ultimately, I think, not entirely clear as to the proper direction of
the humanitarian aid world.

There are many books and articles that are critical and cautionary
with regard to humanitarian efforts, many of them focusing on the
motivation of the people who believe they are helping. Below, I list
and discuss some useful examples.

In *The Road to Hell* Michael Maren writes, "The starving African
exists as a point in space from which we measure our own wealth,
success, and prosperity, a darkness against which we can view our
own cultural triumphs. And he serves as a handy object of our charity.

He is evidence that we have been blessed, and we have an obligation to spread that blessing. The belief that we can help is an affirmation of our own worth in the grand scheme of things." The *Atlantic* article by Teju Cole describing the "white savior industrial complex" is a restatement of Maren's observation. Both Cole and Maren owe debt to a thinker more from my generation, the Austrian philosopher and social critic, Ivan Illich.

In an address to the Conference on InterAmerican Student Projects (CIASP) in Cuernavaca, Mexico, on April 20, 1968, Illich raises the issue of doing unintentional harm, "… the Peace Corps spends around $10,000 on each corps member to help him adapt to his new environment and to guard him against culture shock. How odd that nobody ever thought about spending money to educate poor Mexicans in order to prevent them from the culture shock of meeting you?"

Here Illich anticipates many contemporary critics of so-called voluntourism: "There exists the argument that some returned volunteers have gained insight into the damage they have done to others – and thus become more mature people. Yet it is less frequently stated that most of them are ridiculously proud of their "summer sacrifices." I do not agree with this argument. The damage which volunteers do willy-nilly is too high a price for the belated insight that they shouldn't have been volunteers in the first place."

Another statement from Illich merits a closer look. He points out an unintended and potentially harmful impact of our best-intended acts as we travel abroad to "help." He says to that gathering of Peace Corp volunteers, "By definition, you cannot help being ultimately vacationing salesmen for the middle-class "American Way of Life," since that is the only like you know." Simply stated, we are social beings and we learn elements of culture and life-perspective from each other. We "teach" our culture wherever we go and, at the same time, learn from the cultures we visit.

But there is a major - even critical - asymmetry in that cultural exchange that has been long noted in the anthropological and sociological literature. The most commonly cited example of this symmetry is Lauriston Sharpe's 1952 article "Stone Axes for Stone-Age Australians." What Sharpe points out and others after him have articulated in various ways is that cultural contact will have deep, long lasting and sometimes even 'fatal' consequences for the lesser-developed (technologically) culture. Indeed, the wisdom of Sharpe's article is that you can kill a culture without doing any physical harm to any individuals. You can harm people by infecting them with ideas. Using the disease analogy is, arguably, not analogy at all. There is a growing literature on "viruses of the mind" that presents for compelling arguments.

This recent article by Debora Dunn (Bearing Witness: Seeing as a Form of Service) effectively summarizes many of the messages in James Dawes book That the World May Know. Dunn offers many nuanced cautions and presents some good suggestions specifically in reference to study travel through universities. She encourages us to "think about service in which students do not descend from on high, but rather come alongside." For his part, Dawes presents this thought: "This contradiction between our impulse to heed trauma's cry for representation and our instinct to *protect* it from representation - from invasive staring, simplification, dissection - is a split at the heart of human rights advocacy." He goes on further to state "The disconcerting paradox of humanitarian work is this: It is sometimes impossible to distinguish between the desire to help others from the desire to amplify the self, to distinguish between altruism and narcissism." Challenging words, those.

In conclusion, being a Periclean Scholar is a process that involves constant learning and growing, therefore ongoing reassessment of intent and action both as an individual and as a Class. Please take all of the above as a point of departure for reflection as you move forward in your personal journey as a Periclean and in your collective journey as a Class.

5. The Role of the Mentor

❖

The Periclean Scholars program depends upon the passion and commitment of dedicated faculty Mentors. Over the life of the program, the intent has been to recruit Mentors from all schools and departments on campus, mirroring the diversity of faculty who teach COR 110, The Global Experience. Indeed, this integrative element of the program is seen by many as one if its main contributions to campus life. Becoming a Mentor means playing an altered role in one's home department for a number of years, and hence any commitment decision must be made in conversation with the relevant department chair and dean. The central role of the Mentor is to facilitate learning. Toward this end, the Mentor should encourage each student to bring the skill sets they are learning in their majors to the table as the Class addresses the issue of meaningfully partnering with each other and organizations on the ground in their country/region of focus. All Classes should be run as seminars, with as much student involvement as possible within a rigorous academic setting. Students should own –and perceive that they own - the Class activities to an increasing degree as the Class travels through their three years together.

Being a Mentor for a Class of Periclean Scholars is a multi-year commitment. The faculty person who accepts this role typically needs to be on-campus with their Class all four years, but exceptions can be made with proper planning. The Mentor should work with her/his home department to plan ahead so that maximum use may be made of course reassigned time at least twice during the four year commitment. Starting with the Class of 2011, a modest compensation for extra preparation time is provided to each new Mentor the summer before their Class meets for the first time.

Country/region of focus

Though travel, especially during the winter term of senior year, has historically been part of the program, this is not a requirement. Responding to feedback from both Periclean Scholars and Mentors, beginning in 2010, the new Mentor has the right and responsibility of choosing the country/region of focus for her/his Class. This is done in close consult with the Director. Various models have been used in the past; some Mentors have chosen to focus on a part of the world with which they have deep expertise and/or personal contacts. Others have chosen to embrace the journey of learning and discovery with their Pericleans, and have chosen a country/region based on their (or of the student's) interests and/or a perceived need. Most Classes feel strongly that they would like new Classes to "recycle" their country/region of focus, and indeed the Class of 2013 has revisited Chiapas, Mexico as well as Honduras and Namibia for other Classes. Thus one option for the new Mentor is to go the "recycle" route, and this path clearly has many potential advantages.

Mentoring and scholarly work

In the best case, the faculty Mentor adjusts her/his research and publication plans so as to dovetail as much as possible with the direction(s) of her/his Class. Since the Mentor recruits and chooses the Class members, it is possible to select students with whom collaborations could be developed. Scholarship of teaching and learning (SOTL) research is one obvious possibility, but substantive disciplinary based research is quite possible as well.

Grant writing

The initiatives focused on by each Class typically involve both human and monetary resources, and part of the job of each Mentor is to work with her/his Class to write grants. A good goal to set for each year is to have submitted at least one internal (e.g., Elon's Funds for Excellence) and external proposal (the Director can provide numerous examples). Though the Mentor is welcome to work with the Director to write grants, the best possible scenario is that the students in the Class research funding possibilities and actively contribute to the grant writing process. It is likely that "Pan-Periclean" proposals will be written, and the Mentor may be asked to contribute to these efforts along with her/his Class. In all cases the Mentor should work with the Director to keep both the offices of Institutional Advancement and of Sponsored Programs informed at all stages. Special support from the Office of Sponsored Programs can come in the form of a visit to the Mentor's Class for either general or more specific advice.

Accounting

Once a Class gets formed, fundraising (from on-campus efforts or externally from grants) begins and each Mentor is expected to act as the senior accountant for her/his Class. This role primarily involves working with the Class fundraising and accounting committees and making sure that funds are channeled to the proper accounts and overall good accounting practices become routine for the Class. Additionally, cohorts may choose to select a class accountant. The Director has a modest "Pan-Periclean" account that can be used as per mutual agreement between the Director and the Mentor.

Relationship with the Director

The Director can be as "hands on" as desired/needed by the Mentor, and wisdom or assistance can come from the more established Mentors as well. The Director meets with each Class and Mentor individually throughout the year and, on an as-needed basis. There are meetings between all Mentors and the Director that serve to share ideas, coordinate efforts, and pass on the wisdom from one Mentor to the others. The Director will keep each Mentor informed about all matters Pan-Periclean and serve to facilitate Class related initiatives. Early in the year the new Mentor needs to set a time slot for her/his IDS 225 ("Periclean") class and inform the Director. The Director will pass this information along through the proper channels. The same applies for setting times for PER 351, 352, PER 451, 452, and COR 455, that is, the Mentor should work with the Director to make sure that each Class appears in the university schedule of classes.

Relationship with other Mentors

All of the Class Mentors need to work with each other and the Director to maximize the effectiveness of the overall program and to minimize working at cross purposes at any point (e.g., coordinating the visits of Pericleans-in-Residence). In the early stages, the new Mentor should seek the advice of Mentor's further along in the program and, in turn, provide support and advice to Mentor's behind them, in effect, mentoring the Mentors. The Mentors, accompanied by the Director, meet fortnightly to discuss updates, goals, and seek advice if needed.

Relationship with the Class

Being a Periclean Scholar Mentor is a job with many dimensions. The program is a mix of traditional academic work and social activism, and adding the Classes to one's normal load is demonstratively not like adding other more traditional 2 or 4 semester hour classes. One of the most intense dimensions of the role of Mentor is that you will grow to know these students very closely, and they you. Your relationship with them individually and as a Class is critical, as are their relationships with each other and as a Class. Class dynamics are crucial in large part because much of what happens during their three years together  is as a team. In many ways it is useful to see membership in their Class as sharing significant similarities to other social organizations to which them may belong (e.g., Greek organizations, clubs). Just like with any relationships, the Mentor-Class relationship is best nurtured by openness, free communication, and mutual respect. The Mentor is the pseudo Professor for all Classes, and as such must demand only the highest standards for course work, but at the same time the larger social experience of being a Periclean Scholar must be monitored.

Mentoring Timeline

Year 0: Recruitment

Organization Fair in September

The new Mentor begins her/his duties at the very beginning of the year by having a presence at the annual Organization Fair held on campus (typically the first week of classes) to highlight all student organizations. Reservation of a table and space at this event should be coordinated with the Director. In preparation for this at least two items should be organized.

1. An informational trifold handout should be composed (there are many models from past years that can be found in the Periclean Corner). This trifold should tell the prospective students about the program in general and her/his class specifically, including information on the Mentor-chosen location of focus (e.g., Haiti), the application process, and other information that would attract top notch students

2. A second item to prepare for use at the Organization Fair is an informational poster (up to 3'x5') with much of the same information as the tri-fold, but with perhaps more pictures and attention to an "eye-catching" design. Duplication and all other associated costs for these materials come from the general Periclean budget

At the Organization Fair it would be optimal to have the Mentor present at the table the entire time to meet new students, but typically members of the three standing Classes will person the table, hand out materials to interested students, answer questions, and take down names and email addresses of interested students.

COR pods fall and spring semester

The Director of Core Curriculum will work with the new Mentor to make presentations at pod sessions both fall and spring semesters. At these sessions the Mentor will have time to do a basic PowerPoint presentation about the vision for her/his Class. At these sessions the trifold and poster should be recycled. Trifolds should be given to each student, and a sign-up sheet for future contact should be made available. Models of these presentations are available.

Application process

The Mentor should have her/his application published on the Project Pericles website at the beginning of the year (an example application can be found in Chapter 9.) The Director will facilitate that process. The application process for the Periclean Scholars has several elements. The Mentor is expected to write a prompt for the application "essay" to be written by the student. In the past Mentors have asked applicants to do some reading and research about the country or region of focus and, for example, present an argument for spending Class energies to address a specific issue or issues that the student has identified. These essays have been in the 800-1200 word range.

A second part of the application process is for the student to get her/his COR professor to write a letter of recommendation. In some cases applicants have used other faculty for this duty and this seems to work fine as well. These letters may come in the form of an email or hard copy.

A third and very labor-intensive part of the application process is a face-to-face interview with the Mentor. These interviews should serve both to further educate the applicant about the nature of the program (the long term commitment aspect, the academic focus, and the teamwork nature of the program). The other main purpose is to give the Mentor useful information with which to make informed decisions about which students to select, and as such a standard interview schedule should be followed. These interviews can be short (15 minutes), but in any case given that there may be as many as 70 applicants, this is a massive investment in time. In the past some interviews have been done via Skype or over the phone. The Director can serve as an alternate interviewer and reader of application essays, and can be consulted at any point during the application process.

The entire application process should be done by spring break since the Mentor will need time to make final selections and inform students well before pre-registration for fall classes begins. An email inviting students to be part of the Class should be sent as soon as the decisions have been made. A note should be sent out to students who were not selected as well (templates for both of these letters are available).

Class Size

The program has struggled with the question of, 'How many Pericleans is the right number of Pericleans' per Class? Early on, Classes experienced considerable attrition when our program was not yet well known and students had few incentives to take 8sh of PER courses, which did not count towards any major, or minor. In recent years, the Directors of the International Studies major, Asian Studies minor, Latin American Studies minor, and African/African-American Studies minor have worked with Periclean Scholars. They have to count PER 272 as a Periclean Scholars' course and all 8sh of PER courses toward their respective minors/concentrations, giving students more incentive to complete the series of four 2sh courses.

Recruiting 25 to 30 students can make for a large and somewhat difficult PER 272 seminar to manage. However, given attrition and the amount of students who study abroad for a semester, this number has been the target number of annual recruits.

Induction Ceremony

Typically in the week after pre-registration for fall classes has ended, there will be a formal Induction Ceremony for the new Class of Periclean Scholars. This event is organized and hosted by the second year students (just ending their first year of being Pericleans) and includes, typically, charges from representatives from each standing Class, the Director, and the new Mentor. In the past, a senior administrator (e.g., Provost) has spoken, but this varies from year to year. All new Pericleans are expected to attend. The Mentor should work with the Director and the professors involved to find the best solution to any time conflicts. In some years the new Mentor has handed out material artifacts representative of the country/region of focus as a symbol of their commitment. Every year the new Pericleans are presented with a Periclean Scholar lapel pin by members of the standing Classes. After the ceremony, which typically lasts about an hour, there is a reception for the new Class and a Class picture is taken. Each new Periclean should also be assigned a peer mentor from the Periclean class ahead of them. This time after the ceremony can serve as an opportunity for the students' mentors to meet the new students. The Mentor can also use this time for initial team building and networking.

Moodle

A course Moodle site should be created as soon as the Class is established. In the past, Mentors have had a Class meeting in the weeks just before summer break to get the Class started on their team building, research and fundraising. This site can be used over the summer to get the Class off to a solid start.

Year 1: IDS 225 (4sh)

Syllabus

The Mentor should have the syllabus for this course written well before the beginning of the fall semester and have both the Director and more seasoned Mentors provide direction and feedback (an example syllabus from a past Class is available in Chapter 9). The syllabus should have a rigorous academic component equal or greater than any other 200 level classes she/he teaches, and grading rubrics should be clear, fair and well communicated. Though all Periclean Scholars Classes are a mix of academics and "extracurricular activity," grades should be based predominantly on measurable academic performance. Digital copies of syllabi from all semesters must be sent to the Director at the beginning of each semester.

Course goals

This fall semester course should have several main goals. First, this course should set high academic standards and expectations for reading, writing and analytical thinking. In large part, this semester should be devoted to having the students become knowledgeable of the history, culture, politics, religion, and current events in their country/region of focus. Part of this deep research should be into the various social, political, and/or environmental issues in this region, focusing on their complexities. Finally, this research should lead the students into discussing possible areas of concentration and potential partners on the working on those issue(s) either on location or remotely.

A second main goal of this first semester is team building. Most class time should be spent on academic learning, but time should be set aside to get to know each other through general team building. Nearly every Class has bemoaned the fact that they did not get to know each other very well until junior or senior year and have advised that the process be started earlier and more intentionally. Goals as to what should be accomplished by the end of the semester can be created as a Class. Some Classes have agreed on (1) their issue(s) of focus and (2) the partnerships that they want to develop related to those issues, while others may still be in the process. Midterm and final examinations are encouraged as opportunities both to assess learning and to help clarify foci.

Class structure

From the very beginning of the program, Classes have found it useful and even necessary to organize themselves into various working groups or committees. The Mentor should guide the Class toward an effective organizational structure that will sustain them for their entire career as Periclean

Scholars. Membership and work on these committees should be woven into the course syllabus. Some of the more critical committees include:

- Fundraising and grants
- Accounting
- Publicity (including trifolds, website, posters, etc.)
- Pan-Periclean
- Social (team building)
- Work groups: Many ad hoc committees need to be formed from time to time including:
    - Arrangements for Pericleans-in-Residence
    - Celebrating Periclean Scholars
    - Induction Ceremony
    - "India Week" (for example) Periclean partnerships

Second to the academic learning, which is a primary goal of each Class, an important decision a Class makes is with whom they will partner in their country/region of focus. These partnerships have become an integral part of the Periclean Scholars program, and though it is possible a Class may chose not to follow this tradition, all past and existing Classes would agree that connections to individuals or organizations on the ground in their country/region of focus have been invaluable. The role of the Mentor is to provide direction as to how to create and nurture these relationships and, importantly, how to vet and be vetted by partners. These partnerships can, and often do, lead to the invitation to campus of a "Periclean-in-Residence." Begun in 2003 by the Class of 2006, the Periclean-in-Residence program allows for a short (1-3 week) visit by expert or experts from the country/region of focus who serve as a resource for the Class but also for the great campus community as well (see FAQ related to Pericleans-in-Residence). Every Class of Periclean Scholars has had at least one Periclean-in-Residence during their three years. Funds for these visits are limited, but have been made possible with creative use of both internal and external funds. The Director typically works closely with the Class and their Mentor in arranging these visits.

Local partnerships

Though making and working with partners in the country/region of focus is important for most Classes, working with local partners has been a Periclean Scholar tradition as well. These local partnerships have been modest and lower key in some cases (the Class of 2006 partnered with Alamance Cares here in Alamance County and donated the proceeds from the screening of their narrative film to this organization) but for several Classes these partnerships have been central to their larger goals. The Class of 2011 has linked together via email and the Internet middle school students in rural Sri Lanka with students at Graham Middle School in Alamance County, and the Class of 2012 has linked together adolescent girls in rural India with the Dream Girls program of the Burlington Housing Authority.

Three year plans

Each student and Class should establish a three-year plan during the first semester. The individual student plans should indicate how their major of study and/or other student roles (e.g., Honors Fellow) would be worked into their three-year efforts. The Class as a whole should establish both a mission statement and a three-year plan with specific goals listed. Consider setting goals for fundraising, service hours, student retention, number of SURF presentations, etc. Quantitative goals could supplement the qualitative evaluation, which takes place each semester via the final reflection essay. Both individual and Class three-year plans should remain constant "works in progress" and be revisited on a regular basis at the beginning of each new semester. This can be worked into a writing assignment as part of the course requirements.

Fundraising

As part of the research and writing done by the Class, emphasis should be placed on seeking both internal and external grants to fund initiatives. Though this may seem premature, the exercise of writing grants can serve to clarify both the mission and methods of the

Cookies To Go-Go. April 8th, 8pm-11pm.

Class. Any external grants should go through the Director and the Development Office and should be coordinated with other Pan-

Periclean efforts. Other fundraising efforts (typically internal, e.g., meal card swipes) should be viewed as having two desired goals, to raise funds and to inform the larger Elon community about the country/region of focus and relevant issues. Toward that end, each Class should develop at least one informational trifold explaining the mission of their Class and their various goals. Each Class should have an account number into which funds can be placed under the general Pericles account, and the Director will facilitate this. Funds raised can be used for team building materials (e.g., a Class t-shirt or "bumper" sticker), for specific initiatives or for supporting initiatives of their partner(s). Each Class needs also to establish a website (e.g., org.elon.edu/pericleanscholars20XX) that can include a variety of materials and should grow and expand as the Class matures.

Pan-Periclean responsibilities

Each Class is asked to elect or select two representatives to the Student Steering Committee that meets with the Director fortnightly. Steering Committee members will report actions of their Class to this body and report back to their Class about what the other Classes are doing. Each Class is asked to support the Periclean Blog by writing articles and Class updates.

As Periclean Scholars and members of the Elon University community, our voices carry considerable weight both inside and outside the walls of the campus. To this point, we have not maximized the use of this influence. A thought for future Classes could be to assign each Periclean Scholars Class to write a letter to a decision/policy maker at some level (examples: Members of Congress, Embassy officials, United Nation's representatives, NGO leaders/CEO, persons of influence [e.g., celebrities and/or other high level public figures]). Digital copies of these missives and all responses should be collected by each Class every semester, and we can begin to collect these over the years and semesters thereby, (1) making our voices heard more broadly and (2) learning from experience as to what kinds of communications garner the higher and more effective response rate from the recipients. This assignment can be done individually, as part of a Class or as a whole Class.

All of the "Pan-Periclean" activities described above should be incorporated into the syllabus for the Class in a meaningful manner.

Participation in Pan-Periclean events like the fall "Celebrating Periclean Scholars" and the spring Induction Ceremony should also be part of a Class participation grade.

PER 271 (2sh): Spring semester

Although each Class met unofficially during the second semester of the sophomore year in order to keep activities and momentum moving forward, beginning in 2009, PER 271 was established as a formal 2sh course. Having a structured course allows for more communication, and more intense Class contact. The Mentor, in consultation with her/his Class, will establish a syllabus for the semester.

Induction Ceremony

During the spring semester it has traditionally been the sophomore Class that has organized and hosted the Induction Ceremony for the new Class of Pericleans. A committee needs to be appointed either at the end of fall or very early spring semester to make sure all arrangements are in place for this event.

Lateral entry

Each Class typically begins with a full compliment of students, but attrition does occur for a variety of reasons. Each Class has had students apply for lateral entry into the program, and in most cases these students have been accommodated. The process for reviewing, agreeing on, and inviting candidates is up to the Class, and the Mentor should monitor this closely insuring that proper protocol has been followed. (For more information, see the FAQ.)

Year 2: PER 351 (2sh), PER 352 (2sh)

During the second year of the program the Class needs to maintain emphasis on academic learning about the country/region of focus and the issue(s) that they have decided to pursue. Assignments and reading covering both more in-depth information of the country/region of focus and the issue(s) chosen by the Class are necessary. In past years the Mentor has allowed the Class members to take a more active voice in constructing the course syllabus, setting the agenda for daily classroom activity, and so on beginning in this second year.

One characteristic of the second two years of the program is that the students are increasingly working on their own individual and/or small group projects. That is to say, some course learning is general to all of the Class (e.g., common readings, country/region updates, etc.), but some learning may be specific to individuals or groups. The syllabus can be, for example, imagined as having two sections, one group and one individual. One

model of how to deal with this in the syllabus is to have 50% of the grade be an Individual Syllabus (IS) complete with assignments, due dates, grading rubrics, and so on. To be clear, every IS should have reasonable work output, doable deadlines, and clear grading rubrics. One model for how to proceed with assessment of IS material is to establish a Peer Review Committee (PRC) of 3-5 students who in turn are responsible for tracking the progress of several of their colleagues (and in turn are also tracked by another PRC member), or to have accountability partners assigned to encourage each other and track each others progress. This model must include specific rubrics, deadlines, and so on so that the PRC member or partner can provide feedback both to the student and to the Mentor. In the junior year, Class plans for reaching more long-term goals should be clarified, refined and acted upon. Each Class in the history of the program has chosen different initiatives, but the common denominator among all of the Classes is that they have communicated with and listened to the partners they have developed in their country/region of focus to set reasonable, appropriate and sustainable goals for their Class.

Examples of Class projects

Almost all Classes have put major effort into producing documentaries about their country/region of focus and their chosen issue(s). These projects have ranged from modest (a six-minute video for Habitat for Humanity Zambia produced by the Class of 2009) to the more aggressive (the Class of 2006 produced a four-part

documentary series on HIV/AIDS in Namibia and a short narrative film). Many Classes have devoted themselves to "brick and mortar" projects, and these also range from the  modest (an addition to a school in rural Sri Lanka by the Class of 2011) to the extraordinary (a large clinic, nurses quarters, a drug store and kindergarten all organized and sustained by the Class of 2010). A third example is the organizing of a summit or conference in the country/region of focus. A wide array of other initiatives have been pursued by individual Classes, and in all cases the Mentor should encourage creative new ideas for both Class and individual projects and goals. Each semester, the Class should be updating their mission statement, three-year plans, website, informational trifolds, and other promotional materials.

Semesters abroad

One issue that is perennial with the Periclean Scholars program is that Elon students study abroad a great deal, very commonly for a semester during the junior or even senior year. The tradition has been that the scholar has been "excused" from being a formal part of the Class for these study semesters, but that she/he stays in close contact with their Class via Moodle and/or other social media (GoogleDocs,

Facebook, etc.). In many cases students return from abroad with renewed passion and commitment to their Class initiatives.

Celebrating Periclean Scholars

A major annual Pan-Periclean event is Celebrating Periclean Scholars and historically it has been the responsibility of the junior Class to organize and host this event. Details on how the event has been planned and run are in the FAQ chapter. The Mentor, working with the Director, needs to facilitate the students in their planning so that the event sets the right tone of celebration. This event, in addition to highlighting the activities and accomplishments of each Class, serves also as a recruitment event. First year (and other) students that are interested in learning more about the program are invited. In the past a senior administrator has spoken at this event (Dr. House in 2009 and Dr. Lambert in 2010).

Periclean Scholar of the Year Award

Every year a rising senior is selected to receive the honor of being named "Periclean Scholar of the Year" at the annual Induction Ceremony in the late spring. Early in spring semester of PER 352 the Class needs to decide how that person is selected. The model that has been used for the past several years is that the junior Periclean Scholars decide how to nominate candidates and have them write a letter of support for those students. The final decision of the recipient has then been the responsibility of the seniors, with the Director presiding over the final selection process. This award has been endowed by a gift from the Eugene M. Lang Foundation and supports a $500.00 scholarship for the student selected.

Year 3: PER 451 (2sh), PER 452 (2sh)

The role of the Mentor in the senior year can be very intense, especially depending upon how the Class decides to spend their Winter Term. Everything above describing the role of the Mentor junior year continues in the final year, though there are some additional duties that tend to be placed on the Mentor.

Winter Term travel

Planning for COR 455 should begin in the spring of the junior year, and can involve an on-campus class or a travel-embedded class.

The majority of Classes have chosen to travel to their country/region of focus during Winter Term of their senior year. As mentioned above, this is not a requirement for the program and any decision to travel must be made in the context of making the most effective use of both financial and human resources. To be clear, there should be a detailed plan to accomplish specific and significant goals during this travel. Examples of how to effectively travel to the country/region of focus can be derived from past Mentors, and they can elaborate on what has worked well and not so well in past years. Additionally, information can be found on each Class website (org.elon.edu/pericleanscholars20XX).

The Periclean Scholars program works closely with the Isabella Cannon Global Education Center on these Winter Term study trips, and planning should begin in the early spring of the junior year. Depending upon the nature of the travel and what the intended outcomes are, this can be a full-time effort of the Class and will require constant input from the Mentor. Help will come from the Director on all aspects of this travel as well, and if mutually agreed, the Director can be the second faculty person accompanying the students. Funding for this travel, just like all Winter Term study abroad travel at Elon, comes from the students themselves. A detailed budget that includes absorbing the cost for the Mentor should be generated very early spring semester of the junior year.

For future classes

Consider keeping copies of everything that your Class produces (flyers, articles, e-net announcements, brochures, PowerPoint presentations, etc.) and making these available to future Mentors via a Moodle site or tenure file type folder. You may select a "Class Historian" from your Class to take responsibility for keeping a record of Class efforts and accomplishments. Knowing the ups and downs of other Classes should help current Classes to be stronger and stronger.

Sustainability Committee

As graduation nears, each Class begins to focus more clearly on plans to sustain the partnerships and initiatives begun as undergraduates. A Sustainability Committee (however named) should be organized by each Class as early as first semester senior year, but no later than spring semester. Plans should be made for how to ensure continued communication channels among, and between, Class members, Mentor, Director, and partners. This committee also needs to plan how to continue to support their partners.

Periclean Foundation

The Periclean Foundation, originally named the Periclean Scholar Alumni Association (PSAA), was established in 2006 and functions to maintain cohesion among the alumni. In 2008, the PSAA was endowed by the Redwoods Group Foundation (CEO Kevin Trapani, Elon parent '07), and roughly $5,000 is generated annually. The PSAA had the responsibility to decide how those funds are allocated, and the intent is that they are to be used to sustain the partnerships each Class initiates. Ideally each alumnus commits to contributing to the PSAA so that as more Classes and partnerships accrue, there will be sufficient funds to meaningfully support all partnerships. The Mentor should make sure that her/his Class has a good sustainability plan that includes annual giving through the PSAA.

Final assessment and feedback

Part of the end of the semester should be spent in reflection with the Class on the entire journey. As part of a final examination for PER 452, the students, for example, could be asked to detail what they have learned about themselves, their country or region of focus, their chosen issues and, importantly, the process of working as a team for over three years.

Letters of recommendation

By the nature of the program, it is usually the fact that the Mentor has an intimate knowledge of each student in the Class, perhaps even better than their academic advisor. Thus, one critical role of the Mentor during the senior year is to respond to numerous (likely close to 100% of the Class) requests for letters of recommendation for graduate school or other post-graduate plans such as Teach for America, Peace Corps, etc. Since the Periclean Scholars program is fairly complex but important to describe for these letters, the Mentor can save time by having a standard paragraph written describing the program and the goals of her/his Class in broad outline. Saving these letters to be updated and revised for future requests is advised.

End of year celebration

Each senior Class has organized an event at the end of the school year to celebrate their three years together and the many accomplishments of the Class. The main Pericles budget absorbs the cost of a nice meal for all students and select guests of the Class at this event, and the Director needs to be involved from the beginning stages of planning. Choice of venue, date, and range of people to be included needs to be made very early in the spring. Some Classes have chosen to invite parents and friends to this event, and in that case extra funds would be needed. The Class of 2010 set the precedent of having a fairly elaborate event the Thursday evening before graduation that served as a fundraiser as well.

Graduation

Beginning in 2010, all graduating Periclean Scholars are listed on the official graduation program, and the Mentor must get a complete list to the Registrar (and Director) very early in the spring semester. Every Class has chosen to have some physical representation of their Class displayed on their graduation gowns (e.g., the AIDS pin worn by the Class of 2006 to commemorate their focus on the HIV/AIDS crisis). Beginning with the Class of 2010, stoles have been crafted for the graduating seniors to be worn over the gown. The stoles typically are designed and made in the country or region of focus. For example, the 2010's had theirs designed and made in Ghana, and the 2011's had theirs designed and made in Sri Lanka.

Leaders of the 21st Century

As of 2011, the graduating Class of Periclean Scholars is celebrated at the Leaders of the 21st Century Celebration held early evening on the Friday before graduation. The graduating class is celebrated along with Honors Fellows, North Carolina Teaching Fellows, Isabella Cannon Leadership Fellows, Business Fellows, Elon College Fellows, Lumen Scholars and Communications Fellows. The graduating Class is responsible for providing information for the program, and will be contacted directly about it by another office. Faculty, administration, staff, parents and friends are invited to attend this important event.

Year 4+: Post graduation

Though the formal relationship between the Mentor and her/his Class ends at graduation, it is inevitable that the Mentor will keep in touch with many of the Scholars as they begin their post-Elon lives. For many reasons, communication needs to be maintained between, and among, the Mentors and former students, and the Mentor should work closely with the Director and Alumni Relations to ensure that contact is maintained. The sustainability of the partnerships that have been created is now in the hands of the Periclean Foundation, and the Mentor needs to encourage active involvement in this organization.

Thoughts from Past Mentors

Ghana Class of 2010: Heidi Frontani

The Ghana class made sustainability a focus of their work and this has helped the class to be effective and to continue its projects in Ghana for years after its 29 founding members graduated in 2010. The class has been active for nearly eight years now, with younger members on campus holding meetings, fundraising via meal card swiping and Periclean Card sales, engaging in study abroad in Ghana and other activities and alums involved via monthly group email updates, their own fundraising projects, visits to Ghana, and 'Periclean-style' employment with non-profits and related organizations, and advanced study in sustainability, health, education, and other areas. We have hosted book groups online and several small reunions over meals that have brought alums in contact with newer members.

It is very likely that our class would not have had the successes that we have had, including the construction of a 10-room health clinic that serves hundreds of patients each month and that has a staff that is paid by the Government of Ghana and resides in two blocks of housing also constructed via a partnership between villagers in Kpoeta and the Ghana Periclean class, without the project having been one that was initiated at the request of the community itself. Dr. Francis Amedahe, Dean at the University of Cape Coast in Ghana spent the 2006-07 academic year teaching in Elon's School of Education; he approached the Ghana Pericleans within two weeks of their induction in April 2007 to see if they would be willing to help with the construction of a health facility in his home village of Kpoeta in which 10,000 people had no year round access to health care. Dr. Amedahe then served as the class's contact on the ground. We wired funds we raised and he organized male villagers to build walls and furnishing and female villages to cook meals for the workers. He hired plumbers, roofers, electricians and other experts to complete the specialized work the villagers, who are largely farmers, could not and arranged for the transportation of needed medical and construction items from Accra to Ghana's rural southeastern Volta Region. Dr. Amedahe also arranged for meetings between villagers and Ghana Pericleans who visited over WT and those that completed a semester of study in Ghana.

The Ghana class also very likely would not have had the successes that we have had, including construction underway of a large, multi-room kindergarten in Sokode, Ghana without the support of Africanist and WT Ghana Abroad course founder Dr. Brian Digre, who is an Honorary Chief in Sokode and who has allowed Ghana Pericleans to leave his WT Ghana course to visit Kpoeta for an afternoon each January, after visiting Sokode for a couple of days. Dr. Digre has also assisted with the transportation of donated books and medical supplies from Elon to Norfolk, VA where, through a partnership with the US Navy, all of the items have been transported free of charge.

Finally, the class likely could not have had the successes that we have had without the faculty Mentor having area expertise in Africa and strong academic interest in international development. Due to Dr. Frontani's academic expertise, Ghana Pericleans were able to co-author academic works on Africa or Ghana with her in peer-reviewed publications (the *Oxford Encyclopedia of African Thought* and in the journals *Progress in Development Studies, African Studies Quarterly* and *Africa Media Review*) and in editor-reviewed campus publications including *Visions Magazine*. Eight Ghana Pericleans received Lumen Prizes, five of them for research on Africa or international development (4 in the 2010 Class and 1 in the 2012 Class) and others received fellowships for research on Africa and the diaspora while at Elon or post-graduation.

The Ghana class continues to take on new projects while supporting the health center in Kpoeta and kindergarten in Sokode. In 2013 the class added a domestic initiative, a partnership with the Ghana-Periclean member founded non-profit organization ScholarCHIPS that provides college scholarships to US students with high need. As faculty Mentor I am proudest of the long-term commitment that the Ghana class members have made to our projects (not only our main ones, but also many smaller initiatives including hosting a 3-day Africa festival on campus in Dec. '09, giving support to a Heifer International project in Sokode, raising school supplies for Sokode schools, hosting solar cooker workshops and bringing cookers to Ghana, and creating a partnership with a CA-based non-profit to get used laptops to Ghana) and the recognition and support that we have received from Ghanaians. Dr. Frontani was inducted as an Honorary Chief (Queen Mother) in Kpoeta by the community in 2009, the Government of Ghana added the Kpoeta clinic into its official circuit of facilities receiving Ministry of Health medical supplies in 2011, and by early 2015 Ghanaians (both the Government through salaries and community members through donations and 'durbars' or fundraisers) had contributed $32,000 to our partnerships and projects, out of a total of $163,000 in cash and supplies raised to date.

A final 'take away' message: Doing good work can lead to some amazing things happening that support the partnerships of a Periclean class, without the class or community partners needing to do any of the fundraising. After much encouragement from Dr. Amedahe and the Paramount Chief of Kpoeta (who used to work for Ghana's Highway Department), the Government of Ghana leveled, widened, and paved the approximately 7-mile long road that connects Kpoeta to Kpedze, the nearest village with a somewhat larger health facility; the poor, virtually unusable condition of that road during the rainy season was a major reason the people of Kpoeta had lacked year round access to health care. The improved road now serves the village of Kpoeta in many positive ways—reducing the time and cost for transporting agricultural products, improving access to regional markets, and making Kpoeta a more inviting destination for regional tourists and workers. Within the last year, three students from a university in the Volta Region's largest town, Ho, interned at the health clinic in Kpoeta for a semester.

Central Appalachia Class of 2014: Ken Hassell

One of the most rewarding aspects of becoming a Periclean Mentor was the selection process. Although meeting with almost 70 students was quite intense and time-consuming, the process provided me with insights into what kinds of students were applying for this long-term scholarly and experiential program. The interviews were arranged so that each applicant had 30-45 minutes to present themselves and their concepts of what community service is in a contemporary context. My initial description denoted that these was an 'interviews' when really they were less structured and more like a conversation between two people. I was able to learn a great deal about their motivations and, more importantly, their intellectual thought processes about being open to uncertainty, ambiguity and how deeply they have thought about the unfamiliar and the Other.

It was (and is) important that I insisted on the first domestic Periclean project in the history of the program. Too often, service in distant and more remote areas of the world becomes an exotic and exclusive project that does not recognize human needs in relatively nearby communities. The Pericleans' work in central Appalachia really opened the students' minds to the complex issues of corporate imperialism and resultant oppression, blatant stereotyping, lack of medical and social services as well as education in a region that is a mere 250 miles from our campus. Because of our site's close proximity, we were able to meet many activists, develop close relationships and work in our communities several times each year, sometimes just for a long weekend. These relationships were crucial to understanding that the people of Appalachia were more complexly human and active than their depiction in the media. These life-changing experiences also helped to bring our cohort closer together and inspire democratic ways to help within the communities.

All service learning projects, especially the Periclean Scholars program, should be grounded in *critical* service learning. This means that classroom time and the scholarly element be devoted not just to learning about the people, cultures, politics, and economics of the project region. They must also include extensive readings on postcolonial and anti-essentialistic approaches to taking on this kind of work and making us aware of our privilege, assumptions about other and what is appropriate and normative. This should happen *before* students enter into their community work. There should be an emphasis on how they native people they will be working are often very active in their communities and understand both the issues and politics of what needs to be done. That our role quite often is to listen and learn from the people who live everyday of their lives in their circumstances and are intimately familiar with them. This would be a postcolonial approach to service. We must be careful not to assume that we know better and are more capable of providing 'solutions' than those who live in the region.

The first year of the Periclean Scholars' classes were focused on finding a location, organizations and activists within that location and developing a coherent strategy and theme for moving ahead. It is a messy and often times contentious process that results in schisms within the cohort and even antagonism towards the Mentor and program. While this might seem untenable and antithetical to the Elon image and creating a group that is unified in its intentions, it is necessary in order for students to imbibe how a truly open, inclusive and democratic process works. In other words, the Pericleans must model their classes and approach to developing their work on the egalitarianism that should be the reality in their selected communities. The role of the Mentor is to assure openness and equity within these student conversations and decisions. In one fell swoop, I lost several students who found the initial untidiness and uncertainty of a democratic feminist classroom too foreign to their need for immediate order and control. This must be viewed as simply part of sorting out who is accepting of change, uncertainty and unfamiliarity which is an essential disposition to have when working in a different place with different people.

Haiti Class of 2015: Bud Warner

Without a doubt, the best part of being a Periclean Mentor has been watching my students as they have developed over the past three years. Their insights, understandings, and abilities to think things through have all increased exponentially. While not all of our plans have gone as we wished, their commitment and enthusiasm as a cohort has sustained them. As I look at them on the cusp of their graduation from Elon, I am inspired by their vision of what the future can look like, I am energized by their sense of responsibility to the world, and I am grateful that I had the opportunity to learn so much from them.

6. Pan-Periclean

❖

Opportunities

Work Study

Each semester, approximately two Periclean Scholars will be hired as work-study students. These students can be from any Periclean Class. Tasks include creating programs for events, creating Pan-Periclean posters, working on the newsletter, updating the Pan-Periclean Moodle site, updating the handbook, compiling all information from alumni, assisting with events such as CELEBRATE, and other small tasks regarding the program. In addition, Mentors should feel free to ask the students workers to assist them with small projects for their Classes such as making copies of a Periclean documentary, ordering books for the Class, etc.

For more information, please contact Dr. Arcaro or the Project Pericles Program Coordinator, Catherine Parsons (cparsons@elon.edu).

Periclean Scholars Steering Committee

What is it?

The PSSC is a small group of Periclean Scholar leaders who meet with the Director and/or Associate Director on a fortnightly basis. For example, during 2015's spring semester, they are meeting at 4:00PM the first and third Thursday of the month in the new Periclean Scholars area in Global Commons.

Is this a new initiative?

No. The Steering Committee has been active at some level for most of the existence of the program. The activity level varies depending upon the needs of the program and other variables.

Which Pericleans make up the Steering Committee?

Ideally there are two representatives from each standing Class as well as representatives from other past graduating Classes who have current undergraduate members. All Pericleans and Mentors are welcome to come to these meetings.

How can I become a representative for my Class?

Each Class should determine which two (or three) members would represent their Class. The method for choosing these representatives should be discussed as part of your deliberations on course syllabi. You should make your feelings known if you want to perform this service "officially" and, in any case, all Pericleans are welcome to come to the meetings and provide input.

What is the overall purpose of this body?

The central mission of the Steering Committee is to further communication, coordination and planning between both Classes and the Director.

Who sets the agenda for the regular meetings?

Any Periclean or Mentor can present agenda items for these meetings. The Director or Associate Director has historically set the general agenda.

What typically happens at these meetings?

Reports are issued from each Class and from the Director. Representatives give updates on activities, partnerships, grant writing initiatives and so on. The Director passes on an update on her/his activities and typically facilitates the meeting. Additionally, Pan-Periclean activities are discussed (e.g., Induction Ceremony) and plans are clarified.

Does this body have a budget?

There is no specific budget set aside for the Steering Committee, but the Director has a budget that is to be used for supporting the program. If the Steering Committee decides that there are materials or activities (e.g., Pan-Periclean breakfast bagels and coffee) that are appropriate use of funds then the Director frees up the resources to make it happen.

What are the duties of the Class representatives to the Steering Committee?

The Class representatives are to take notes at the meeting and present the updates learned at the meeting at their next regular Class meeting. Additional duties include working on Pan-Periclean initiatives and providing support both for other Classes and the program as a whole.

Do Class representatives get credit or a grade for their work on the Steering Committee?

Mentors are encouraged to include Pan-Periclean activities in their syllabi and to that extent the work is evaluated and credit is given. Being a member of the Steering Committee is a significant service to the program and is deeply valued.

Events

Celebrating Periclean

What is 'Celebrating Periclean Scholars?'

Begun in 2010, the Celebrating Periclean Scholars event is typically held fall semester and is designed to honor the current and past Periclean Scholars. It is also an opportunity for prospective first year students to learn about the program. This is intended to be a "bookend" event to the Induction Ceremony in the spring and thus a Pan-Periclean gathering in which all Classes come together and present their vision and accomplishments.

How do people learn about this event?

Pericleans learn about the event through normal channels (e.g., emails from the Director, the Steering Committee, etc.). Publicity for the event targeting first year students can be arranged via numerous avenues: flyers, Moseley table handouts, digital posters, and so on.

What happens at the actual event?

Though each year is slightly different, the overall structure traditionally has featured short update speeches from each current Class, an address by the Director and/or Associate Director, a special alumni speaker, and, in the past, we have had keynote speakers from the administration. Elon's President, Provost, and Associate Provost have all made an address in recent years. The

event sometimes begins with an icebreaker and typically ends with a reception and food from one or more of the countries of focus. Most years some Periclean-logo 'swag' has been given to all Pericleans and guests (e.g., water bottles).

Is there a budget for this event?

Publicity, food, programs and swag are all covered by the main Periclean budget. Any major items should be cleared through the Director and reimbursement is made by turning receipts into the Program Coordinator Catherine Parsons (if over $150.00) or signed by the Director and taken directly to the Bursar's office (if under $150.00).

Who is in charge of this event?

Traditionally the junior Class of Pericleans has taken leadership on this event and a representative from this Class act as Master of Ceremonies throughout. This Class works closely with the Director to organize the event, create and print the program, secure the speakers, order and distribute swag, arrange for the set up and teardown of the venue, making sure that all multimedia needs are met, host the reception (including ordering the food, etc.) and other details to insure a smooth event.

Elon University

Celebrating Periclean Scholars

Wednesday, October 29, 2014

"Creating and sustaining meaningful global partnerships since 2003"

Welcome and Introduction
Arianna Brown, Class of 2017

Thoughts from the Director
Dr. Tom Arcaro

Class Updates
Class of 2017: Susan Reynolds and David May
Class of 2016: Abby Senseney
Class of 2015: Cat Palmer and Elaina Vermeulen

Presentation of Elevator Videos

Introduction of Featured Speaker
Mary Frances Foster

Keynote Address
Samantha White '06

Closing Remarks and Reception Invitation

We also invite you to the Restavek Freedom Foundation Benefit Concert starting at 9:00 PM at the West End Terrace.

How are keynote and alumni speakers scheduled?

Special guests have been contacted well in advance of the event and have been asked to speak between 3-7 minutes. The point of contact can be the Director or the chairperson of the Planning Committee.

What are the various "to-do" items for the Planning Committee?

- Secure venue
- Secure all special speakers and representatives from each Class to speak
- Lie out and have printed program (nice cardstock) for event. Arrange to have these handed out at the beginning of the evening as people arrive
- Secure all technology needs
- Order swag
- Advertise event to first year students
- Organize food for reception
- Organize all set up and clean up
- Appoint, "Master of Ceremonies" for the event
- Coordinate with Director/Associate Director and Steering Committee on all of the above details

What about event assessment?

Within a week after the actual event the Planning Committee should meet and assess the evening and make recommendations for changes for the new year. These recommendations should go to the Director and be incorporated into an updated FAQ.

Awareness Weeks

The Awareness weeks are typically weeks picked out by each individual Class in the spring (March/April), where they promote their projects and awareness of their country through activities such as speakers, movie sponsoring, and video screenings. Awareness weeks are catered to fit the needs and wants of each individual Periclean Class.

Panels/Speakers

When arranging panels and speakers, be sure to advertise the event and use SPACES to book the space that will be used for the speaker. You will be in charge of contacting the speakers you wish to have. If the speaker is external (author, columnist, documentary film maker etc.), then you will need to arrange accommodations for them, including logistics of housing, receptions, and dining for after and before the panels, and any other necessary booking. If the panel is designed to bring awareness toward your issue, then look towards inviting faculty members on the panel who are specialized in your area. Ensure that the Elon University community is aware of the panels and speakers since often times other departments, such as international studies and communications, are interested in helping fund and participate in these events.

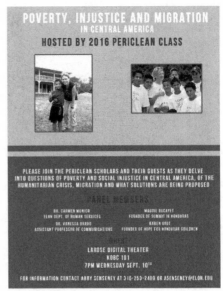

5K Fundraiser

Planning a Periclean 5K can be time-consuming given the scope of the logistics, community outreach, and advertising necessary to make the event a success. Having a dedicated committee and well-organized plan will go a long way in streamlining the process. Based on previous experiences, a month-by-month timeline has been compiled and is included in the FAQ section. Feel free to adapt the guidelines to make them work for each Class. Just remember – the earlier a Class starts planning, the better!

7. Frequently Asked Questions

❖

Several years ago, in order to better organize Periclean Scholars, we began writing frequently asked questions documents to have a better understanding of the program including:

I.   Finances
II.   Finance Tips
III. Becoming a Periclean as a Fellow
IV. Lateral Entry
V.   Periclean-in-Residence
VI. Periclean Newsletter
VII. Periclean World Corner
VIII. Periclean Graduation Sashes
IX. Periclean 5K Fundraiser

I. Finances

Budgets

Until recently Periclean Scholars Classes have been responsible for raising virtually all of their own programming funds. Before 2015 no Class was given a 'starting budget,' although funds for creating application materials, induction ceremony programs, and senior dinners have been made available. Most Classes have opted to create a Class T-shirt and program funds potentially can be borrowed and repaid when students receive and pay for their shirts.

There are several accounts for the Periclean Scholars. Each is a joint account for all Periclean Scholars Classes. Thus, it is imperative that your accountant for your Class document each deposit and withdrawal very carefully. You should not be accessing Periclean Scholars funds without checking with Dr. Arcaro first unless they are funds that your Class raised and deposited.

Accounting:

Get a receipt:

Always indicate "Class of XXXX" or "XXXX Pericleans" on transactions, replacing XXXX with the year of graduation for your Class, and getting a receipt. The Bursar's Office prints out a receipt for you on the spot. University Advancement will print out a record of deposits to the account for a given time frame.

Say Thank You

It is good practice to have a student who can work with the accountant to collect names and addresses of donors to send out thank you notes.

Each Class of Periclean Scholars has used a variety of approaches to raise money for projects. Grant writing, letter writing campaigns, working with local restaurants, swiping Phoenix cards for Phoenix cash or Meal Plan dollars, craft sales, video sales, having donation buckets at events or tables at College Coffee or Moseley Center, etc. have all been used. What follows is an assessment of how well each of these approaches has worked to date as well as some details on the logistics.

Accountant Handbook

The accountant will be responsible for each of the following duties over term(s) in office:

- Making deposits and withdrawals from University accounts
- Maintaining a written and/or electronic record of all account activity, donations, expenses, etc.
- Reporting funds to the Class when necessary and monitoring the allocation of funds to individual classmates as well as the group
- Collecting, copying and recording all receipts for purchases by individuals. Creating a "master accounting book" is highly advised for a central location for all necessary documents
- Counting money at various fundraising events and sorting bills and rolling coins for deposit when necessary

Note: Each of these duties will be outlined further in following pages.

VERY IMPORTANT:

These account numbers will be required for withdrawals and deposits. Be sure to make known to the Bursar that you are depositing or withdrawing from "the Periclean Scholars Class of _____" as all of the Periclean accounts are lumped together and the money will not be allocated to the proper Class unless the Bursar is notified.

General Responsibilities: Maintaining a written or electronic record of all account activity is imperative to the success of the organization. To abide by the Elon Honor Code, following University policies and procedures is of utmost important when acting in the role of accountant.

Bursar

In order to deposit funds, one must first total all cash and check amounts. Organize the money in a proper fashion to give to the Bursar's office for deposit. Visit the Office of the Bursar in Alamance building 111 in order to complete the transaction. When giving monies to the attendant, BE SURE to note that your funds are for "the Periclean Scholars Class of _____." Currently, Periclean Scholars as a whole has one main account, and the funds are allocated to each Class as noted on deposit slips. In order for YOUR Class to receive the proper amount, this information must be made known at the time of the deposit.

You will receive a receipt for the funds from the bursar attendant. It will note the amount received as well as the party that made the deposit. Correct the deposit if your receipt does not say "Periclean Scholars (YEAR)." You may either ask the bursar attendant to make a copy of this receipt or accomplish the task yourself. This receipt and its copy must be filed in the accounting master book, as well as in the overall master book, kept by the Mentor.

University Advancement

Should your Class receive a grant from Elon University, an Institutional Advancement account may be set up for you. Deposits are made in a similar fashion if necessary, by visiting the Bursar in Alamance building 111. However, a set amount of money, in the amount of your grant, will be provided initially in the account, and you will primarily make withdrawals from this type of account.

All checks are sent to University Advancement so that the donor can get a receipt for tax purposes (as long as they gave the money as a direct donation rather than receiving t-shirts, Ghana cards, etc.).

Withdrawals

Various types of withdrawals can be made from Bursar and University Advancement accounts. Cash withdrawals can be made in order to reimburse the Mentor, an individual or third party. This should be for small or trivial amounts.

Two other types of withdrawals, check requests, and wire transfers, require additional forms to be completed. Check request forms are included in the appendix of this document, and one must email Catherine Parsons at cparsons@elon.edu in order to get a typed wire transfer form for submission.

Following are detailed instructions for each of the check request and wire transfer processes:

- Completing a check request is a fairly simple process. Ask Catherine Parsons (cparsons@elon.edu) to email you a blank check request form. Once you have a blank form, fill it out with the necessary information (name, address, account numbers, amounts, and identification numbers). Be sure to include a description of what the money was used for in order to keep proper documentation.
- A signature is required for the check request to be processed in all cases.
- For amounts of up to $999, the director of Project Pericles, Dr. Tom Arcaro, may authorize payment. Visit his office in Global Commons 210 and contact him before hand. This form may then be submitted to the Accounting Office via campus mail (Campus Box 2900) or in person.
- The office is located at 314 Haggard Avenue, near the Arts West building.
- For amounts over $1,000, the Associate Provost must approve withdrawal. Once the form is signed, it may be submitted once again to the Accounting Office at 314 Haggard Avenue. Catherine Parsons is happy to help with the check request process.
- Again, make copies of these forms, as they will serve as receipts for such transactions. File these copies in both the accounting master book as well as the overall master book with your Mentor.

Wire Transfer

Completing the process for a wire transfer is a bit more complicated than a check request. It is highly advised to transfer as much money as possible to avoid multiple wire transfer requests and make the transaction as efficient as possible.

To obtain a wire transfer request form email Catherine Parsons. She will type up the form for readability and acceptance for the Accounting office. Once this form is obtained make sure to have the proper authorization as follows.

For amounts of up to $999, the director of Project Pericles, Dr. Tom Arcaro, may authorize payment. Visit his office in Global Commons 210 and contact him beforehand. The wire transfer may then be submitted to the Accounting Office via campus mail (Campus Box 2900) or in person. The office is located at 314 Haggard Avenue, near the Arts West building.

For amounts over $1,000, the Associate Provost must approve withdrawal.

Again, make copies of these forms, as they will serve as receipts for such transactions. File these copies in both the accounting master book as well as the overall master book with your Mentor.

II. Finance Tips

Stay Organized

The more organized, the better. Record keeping is imperative to show proof of proper handling of monies that pass through the organization.

Inform Your Peers

Keep the Class and fundraising committee updated on the status of funds, fundraising ventures and other financial issues that may arise. Your Class may want to use funds to support a Class bonding event or other experience. Be sure to vote on the allocation of funds as it pertains to your project and other supported endeavors.

Carefully Handle all Monies

All cash and checks should be kept in a safe place, away from a situation where it could be taken or misplaced. Deposits should be made swiftly as to keep minimum liability upon the accountant to handle funds. The Class of 2010 raised over $40,000, a great deal of responsibility for the accountant.

Don't Wait Until the Last Minute

Money does not transfer quickly especially with check requests and wire transfers. Be sure to begin these processes as soon as possible.

Fundraising

Slower, but generally steady income via swiping Phoenix cards for Phoenix cash:

Fill out a form at the Moseley front desk providing information about why you would like to request a table or use the SPACES online system to request the same. Only certain tables have outlets for the Phoenix cards (tables 7, 8, and 9) at Moseley, so indicate that you need one of these tables on your form. Once your table has been approved you will receive an email indicating approval.

You must reserve the Phoenix card-swiping machine separately, through the Phoenix card office near the mail center in Moseley. You may not have the card-swiping machine for more than three days in the same week. The machine comes in a plastic bin and has all the directions on it for use.

Faster, more lucrative but limited to once a year swiping Phoenix cards:

Contact Aramark/dining services EARLY in the semester or term to request approval for swiping Phoenix cards for meal plan dollars. A very limited number of groups will be approved, so ask early! Each swipe will take $2 off a student's card and Aramark will donate up to

$1000 per approved student organization engaged in swiping Phoenix cards for meal plan dollars. If approved for this activity, then go through the same steps for requesting a table at Moseley as described above. Note: the meal swiper is a very expensive (around $6,000) device and it is very important that the students using the device return it to the Dining Services office in Colonnades (rooms 101/108).

Slower and somewhat reliable funds via information tables with a donation bucket (at College Coffee, Moseley Center, Holly Hill Mall):

Like Phoenix cash swiping, these approaches can be expected to bring a few hundred dollars at best after several days of effort involving considerable planning to staff the tables based on everyone's busy schedules. The positive aspect of these approaches is that although the income is not great, they tend to be a fairly reliable ways of bringing in small amounts of money.

Not guaranteed, but potentially larger sums via grant writing:

This approach can be a means of securing somewhat larger sums (thousands versus hundreds). For individual Classes to date, grants have come from the campus level, via the Project Pericles office in New York or through students having personal connections to someone at a foundation. The Fund for Excellence grants via Arts and Sciences (which can be as much as $5,000 for speakers, cultural festivals, etc.), Community Project Initiative Grants, and the Civic Engagement Course Enhancement Grant via Project Pericles and Elon (each gives $2,000 for $4,000 total) are some of the more realistic possibilities. The Director for Project Pericles has secured $125,000 from a local group of businesspeople and these funds have endowed the Periclean Alumni grants for which individual Classes can apply (around $1,000 per Class at this point).

Perhaps the largest sums available via grant writing will be through the Lumen Prizes first awarded in spring 2008. Fifteen Lumen Prizes will be awarded to students in their sophomore year each year. In 2008, Pericleans received five of the 15 Lumen Prizes ($75,000), however, most of this money is slated for tuition remission for individual prizewinners and the remaining funds go into the purchase of equipment, books, airfares, and other personal perks for prize recipients. Thus, the Lumen Prizes are really a wonderful means of highlighting the scholarly aspect of Periclean Scholars (via eventual SURF, NCUR and other national conference presentations and publications), but not an effective means for a Class to raise considerable funds for development projects.

For the most part, longer term approaches to gaining relatively small sums, via the sale of videos, CDs, pins, postcards, artsy blank cards, school bonds, crafts, etc.: Whereas fundraising via the Phoenix Card swiping unit is relatively rapid and virtually guaranteed IF you can be one of the few groups to get the swiping device, obtaining funds via other approaches is often much slower and for the most part should essentially be viewed as part of outreach and education rather than fundraising.

The 2006's made several videos and a CD, and were able to make up for the funds that were invested within a five-year period. The 2007's designed an enamel pin with the Periclean logo and Elon's name on it, but these have been given as gifts to graduating Pericleans and incoming Pericleans. Like videos and CDs, the pin served as a means of outreach and education more so than fundraising. The 2008's had a school bond campaign, but found few buyers for them or their postcards. These were inexpensive experiments, which required little investment of funds. The 2009's worked with a Zambian artist who waived the rights to her artwork so that all of the funds raised could go towards Habitat for Humanity housing in Zambia. This approach has been successfully combined with Elon's purchase of hundreds of sets of blank cards and envelopes as gifts at the 2008 SURF banquet and end-of-the-year faculty luncheon. This was arguably the best model to date for somewhat larger scale (few thousand dollars) fundraising. The 2010's have sold craft items (headbands, necklaces, wallets, tote bags, etc.) made from fabric obtained in Ghana. Even with several 2010 Pericleans having craft making and sewing skills, sales have been modest and the time put into making the crafts and the cost of the cloth are such that craft sales can hardly be considered part of fundraising. Similarly to videos, enamel pins, and school bonds though, these craft items were more of a form of outreach and education.

The Class of 2010 implemented an innovative project beginning in Fall 2008. For the first time, a discount card was offered for purchase to students, faculty, staff and the Elon community. Partnering with local businesses, members of the Fundraising Committee contracted with twelve businesses to donate a discount to the Periclean Scholars Class of 2010. These discounts were then printed on a plastic card, which was the size of a credit card. The discounts were valid for an entire calendar year (January to December 2009). Each business agreed to give the customer a discount when the card was presented at the time of purchase. As a committee, we allowed businesses to decide what discount they would give. A list of companies and their respective discounts as well as the design of the card is included with this document. This project helped raise $2,000 toward the development of a health care center in rural southeastern Ghana.

III. Becoming a Periclean as a Fellow

Can I become a Periclean Scholar if I am a Fellow (Leadership, Honors, Business, Elon College, Communications, Teaching)?

YES! Since the Periclean Scholar program began with the Class of 2006, many Periclean Scholars have been also been involved with other University Fellows programs including Honors, Leadership, Business, Teaching, and Elon College.

How can I do all of the work demanded by my Fellows program and be a Periclean Scholar?

Following guidance from their Mentor, Periclean Scholars choose a major focus for their Class, typically (though not necessarily) featuring meaningful partnerships with international entities, e.g., Habitat for Humanity International and the Heifer Project. Based on this broad focus, they establish individual and Class goals, both short and long term. Each Periclean Scholar is encouraged to "double-dip" on major projects both within their major and other programs with which they may be involved. Though "double-dipping" may not be possible or desirable in all cases, if done with proper planning and coordination between the student, her academic advisor, the Periclean Scholar Class Mentor, and the Fellows advisor, it can work effectively.

How do I apply to become a Periclean Scholar?

The application process takes place in Spring semester of your first year. There are three components to the application: a letter of recommendation from a faculty person, a letter of application, and an interview with the Class Mentor. Applicants are notified of their acceptance prior to preregistration for Fall semester.

What courses do I need to take as a Periclean Scholar?

- Sophomore year: IDS 225 4sh, Fall semester
- Junior year: PER 351 2sh, Fall semester; PER 352 2sh Spring semester
- Senior year: PER 451 2sh, Fall semester; COR 455 4sh, Winter Term; PER 452 2sh, Spring semester

Total semester hours: 16

Are there exceptions to the required courses?

Yes. First, many Periclean Scholars choose to study abroad for a semester, and thus miss one of the 2sh junior or senior year courses. This does not impact their status as a Periclean Scholar.

Since there has always been lateral entry into the Periclean Scholars program, that means taking all of the classes as a prerequisite to be a Periclean Scholar is not practical. Also, because a majority of Periclean Scholars go abroad for a semester, that limits the numbers of Periclean Scholars classes that can be taken as well. Given both of those, it has always been a Class decision, in consultation with the Mentor and the Director, as to who would graduate with the official label of Periclean Scholar.

IV. Lateral Entry

What is lateral entry?

Each Class is selected in the spring of their first year and then inducted in a pan-Periclean ceremony typically in the first weeks of April. Lateral entry is where a student(s) is accepted into the program after the official invitations have been sent and the Induction Ceremony has been completed.

Why does lateral entry exist?

Lateral entry exists for several reasons. First, with few exceptions each Class of Pericleans has experienced some level of attrition and has felt a need to replenish its numbers. Though we make every attempt to broadcast the opportunity to become a Periclean Scholar, there are always some students who only become aware and interested in the program after their Class has been selected. Thirdly, there have been numerous times in our history when special circumstances arose making adding new Class members clearly beneficial.

Who decides whether a Class takes lateral entry students?

This has always been a Class decision made in consultation with the Mentor and the Director. The Class decides the timing and more importantly the process. To be clear, lateral entry of students not in the same Class year is being phased out.

How are lateral entry students identified?

There are a number of ways Classes have experienced dealing with lateral entries. In many cases, Class members are approached by non-Periclean students (frequently classmates, friends, or co-members of other affiliation groups on campus) who show an interest in the program or the particular issue being addressed by the Class. As frequently the case will be that Class members will seek out recruits through this same kind of networking. A third method is through active recruitment on campus using various social

PERICLEAN SCHOLARS: APPALACHIAN CLASS
LATERAL ENTRY "APPALCATIONS"

http://periclean.wordpress.com/documents
email to rmcfarland2@elon.edu by may 3

social change   civic engagement   meaningful partnerships

networking mechanisms (e.g., Facebook, posters on campus, and so on).

Has it always been that way?

Some past Classes have had lateral entry from other class years. Though many Classes in the past have had "friends of the Class of 20XX" that were an additional support system for the Class and were from various graduation years, the Class of 2010 has had a lateral entry system - now being phased out - whereby that Class Mentor worked with small groups of students who were "officially" Pericleans. The Class of 2012 also has a lateral entry student.

How can a Periclean Class sustain their initiatives without recruiting younger lateral entries?

The responsibility of every Periclean Class is make efforts to sustain the partnerships they created as undergraduates long after graduation, and this can be accomplished in various ways. After graduation the onus is on the alumni Pericleans to maintain contact with each other, remaining undergraduate "friends," their partner(s), their Mentor and the program Director in order to meaningfully sustain their initiatives and partnerships. Additionally, the program is now intentionally "recycling countries/regions of focus (e.g., the 2016's are going back to Honduras, also the focus of the '07's, and the 2017's will reconnect with Namibia, the country of focus for the '06's), thereby providing pathways to maintain contacts and partnerships from one generation of Pericleans to the next.

How do lateral entry students "catch up" with their Classmates?

This is a Class decision, but the history is that lateral entry students are asked to do remedial work about the country of focus and the issue(s) being worked on by the Class.

Can a student become a Periclean Scholar as late as their senior year?

The best-case scenario is to have lateral entry students come in as juniors, but there have been exceptional cases in the past where lateral entries have started as late as first semester seniors. The later the student joins a Class, of course, the more remedial work should be required.

Are lateral entry students "official" Pericleans?

Yes. This means that they take all of the PER classes, are active in their Class, and thus appear on the Class roster for the Leaders of the 21st Century program and on the official graduation program.

V. Pericleans-in-Residence

Each year the sophomore Class will have the option to host their first set of Pericleans-in-Residence, which encompasses approximately a week long stay of guests native to or residing in the Class's country of focus. The Class should plan the schedule of their stay from the time of their arrival to the time of their departure, including housing, food, and transportation to and from the airport. It would also be great to plan an activity open to the Elon community in order to spread awareness and get the Periclean Scholars' name out there. In addition, it will be a wonderful learning opportunity for Pericleans as well as the University as a whole.

The Periclean-in-Residence has become an integral and even transformational dimension of the Periclean Scholars program, with each new Class bringing in guests to help them understand their chosen topic much more clearly. The four Pericleans-in-Residence that the Class of 2006 hosted (Drs. Philippe Talavera and Lucy Steinitz, Anita Isaacs, and Majiua Marigulala) helped define and focus this Class' mission and in no small fashion contributed to the success of the documentary series on HIV/AIDS in Namibia. Karen Godt, the Periclean-in-Residence hosted by the Class of 2007, continues to have an impact on that Class and on the Elon community as a whole; her daughter is in the Class of 2011. The other Periclean Scholars Classes have similarly benefited from this program. The 2008s invited Peter Brown of the Schools for Chiapas; 2010s invited Dr. Augustus Vogel, Director of Atidekate an organization for Returned Peace Corps Volunteers who worked in Ghana, and Dr. Roger Gocking, a historian of Ghana from Mercy College in New York.

In addition to spending time with the Class that invited them, every effort is made to offer the resource of these Pericleans-in-Residence to the larger campus community and to the large surrounding community. Speaking engagements both on and off-campus have been a regular part of this program.

Who qualifies as a Periclean-in-Residence?

In the past, a Periclean-in-Residence has been someone who is an expert in the field of study either due to their own research or personal experience with the issue. She or he should be able to provide insight into the issue, the severity of the issue and why it is important and, possibly, present new information and a new way of looking towards the problem. This person should also be comfortable speaking in front of audiences of all sizes and be incredibly passionate about the issues at hand.

How do you contact them?

A Periclean-in-Residence can be initially found through personal contacts or networking. Once an appropriate candidate is found, one should call, email, or send a written letter telling the person about you, your organization, and why you are interested in having them speak.

How can their presence benefit the campus?

A Periclean-in-Residence not only greatly benefits the entire Elon University staff and student body, but also the local community at large. Especially since Elon prides itself on being a global community, having a Periclean-in-Residence speak can provide information on issues going on in the world that should be of significance to everyone. Pericleans-in-Residence can use their knowledge and presence to greatly impact and educate people in various organizations and can be a call to action to both students and staff involved in an issue.

What types of audiences will they appeal to?

Especially if the Periclean-in-Residence has different themes they can discuss each night, he or she will appeal to a wide range of audiences. This audience includes local community organizations with similar missions, empowered groups of Elon organizations/clubs, specific academic departments and majors, or even simply to individuals with an interest in the subject matter.

What events can be held with a Periclean-in-Residence?

There can be a wide range of events held. The main purpose of the Periclean-in-Residence is to benefit the Elon community. This includes attending Classes, speeches to large groups, discussion panels, and question and answer sessions. In addition, a Periclean-in-Residence can be involved in community events related to the issue like fundraisers.

How long can they stay?

A Pericleans-in-Residence should stay long enough to fulfill their purpose of teaching various aspects of an issue to a wide range of people and organizations. A week and a half to two weeks would be an appropriate time period.

Where do they stay?

In the past the Pericleans-in-Residence have stayed with students, however if this makes them uncomfortable, a hotel would be the best option.

Where does the funding come from?

Funding the visit of a Periclean-in-Residence can come from limitless places. It is imperative to tap into all of your resources. Often other academic departments who would be interested in sharing the Periclean-in-Residence with their students will be more than happy to co-sponsor.

How do you schedule them?

Make sure you contact the Periclean-in-Residence in advance to finalize their schedule. Double check with Elon, as well, to make sure they are scheduled for when they are suppose to be scheduled. It is important to have the Periclean-in-Residence's schedule pretty structured with events before they arrive, but still leave some room for flexibility if other opportunities arise.

Do they get paid/ How do you thank them?

They have not been paid in the past, but their plane ticket has been purchased for them and on the ground expenses have been covered. A Periclean-in-Residence makes a great personal sacrifice to travel and come to Elon, so it is necessary to thank them accordingly. Personal mementos, such as a scrapbook of their visit to show off their accomplishments, are an excellent gesture. The 2010's used minor fundraising to give Anita Isaacs a $250 for her HIV/AIDS organization in Namibia and purchased some crafts from her; they also have created a $100 honorarium to Dr. Gocking, and several hundred dollars to Dr. Vogel's organization for the purchase of children's books in the village in Ghana in which he served as a Peace Corps volunteer. Our guests appreciated these gestures.

Do they need transportation?

She or he would probably need a student to several student volunteers to be willing to chauffeur them around. It would be helpful if a sign-up sheet were made previous to her/his arrival. This method is helpful for several reasons in that it takes the responsibility off of one sole person to transport her/him everywhere and it helps organize in that everyone will know who is in charge when.

How do you get Global Classes involved?

In the past, we have assigned students to go and speak to different Global Classes.

Where do they hang out?

They can hang out with students, on-campus, etc. We have hosted several activities for past Pericleans-in-Residence such as lunches and dinners with students and even trips to the State Fair and Chapel Hill. Again, it is probably a good idea to make a sign-up sheet to finalize the students' responsibilities for the Periclean-in-Residence's stay.

What time of the year do they come?

Time of year depends on what works best for the speaker as well as Elon's schedule.

How do you prepare for their arrival?

- Decide where they will stay
- Make a schedule of activities (academic and entertainment)
- Make a list of questions to ask them to become more knowledgeable on the subject
- Everyone should be caught up on the subject so there are questions to ask
- Advertise their coming and events and what will be happening at each event

How far in advance should you invite him/her?

We recommend around 2 or 3 months in advance in order to provide him/her with time to prepare as well as to have more options open in the campus calendar. It also allows the Periclean-in-Residence enough time to make appropriate arrangements and for the Class to prepare for hotel and flight reservations.

How do you promote events?

Take advantage of all of the on-campus marketing tools! These include:

- E-net
- Electronic posters in Moseley
- Advertising at a Moseley table
- Flyers around campus
- Student speakers coming to Classes
- E-mail list servers (different organizations, facstaff, etc.)
- WSOE
- ELN

Who do you invite to events?

There can be a wide range of groups to invite to different events during the course of the Periclean-in-Residence's visit. These can include the following:

- The whole campus
- Certain Classes/majors
- Closed group events with just the Periclean Scholars
- Outside campus events/community/cultural events

VI. Periclean Newsletter

How long has there been a Periclean Newsletter?

The Class of 2006 started a newsletter their junior year, though there were only a few issues by the time they graduated. Other Classes took up the idea with varying degrees of success between 2007 and 2009 when the Class of 2011 rejuvenated the idea. At the moment, no Class has taken this project on.

How often does this publication come out?

This has varied over the

years, but the goal has been to put out approximately six per year.

Are there themed issues?

Yes, a typical year would look like this: (1) early September issue highlighting events over the summer and alumni news, (2) early November issue covering fall events and featuring the Celebrating Periclean Scholars gathering in October, (3) late December covering end of semester news and accomplishments, (4) late February issue reporting on Winter Term activities and early semester news, (5) late April issue featuring the Induction Ceremony, and (6) a post-graduate special issue featuring the graduating Class.

Who is in charge of this project?

There had always been student ownership of the newsletter, though the Director was typically the final editor. The optimum structure was to have members from at least two Classes work together on the newsletter.

Do Pericleans that work on the newsletter get "credit" for this work?

How the job of working on the newsletter has figured into the course syllabus and/or course grade has varied from Class to Class, but the intent is that writing done for the newsletter is clearly part of your class participation.

Who can submit articles?

Each Class should have a "Class update" article in each issue, and beyond that, any Periclean is welcome to submit news and/or feature articles as they wish.

Can alumni and partners be featured and/or submit articles?

Yes! In fact this is one of the more important dimensions of the newsletter.

Can photographs be submitted?

Yes, definitely. Art of any sort always makes the publication more inviting for readers. Typically a caption and/or explanation need to accompany any photo that is submitted.

Can my article include hyperlinks?

Yes. Hyperlinks can be included since the vast majority of readers get their copy of the newsletter digitally in PDF format.

Who gets the newsletter?

Digital copies are sent to all current and alumni Pericleans, all current and past partners of Periclean Classes, friends of the program both inside and outside of Elon (e.g., Dr. Lambert here at Elon and Kevin Trapani of the Redwoods Group in Raleigh). Pericleans are urged to forward the newsletter to family and friends, and hard copies of the newsletter are put on display in various places on campus.

What is the purpose of the newsletter?

There are many reasons to produce a high quality newsletter. First, the newsletter serves to create a deeper sense of connection among the existing Classes and to sustain the sense of connection to the program of the Periclean alumni. Secondly, the newsletter serves to educate all of the non-Pericleans about the world. Periclean Class projects (past and present) cover many countries around the world and important issues that impact the people in those countries. Every time a parent or sibling looks at the newsletter they are learning more about the world and hence becoming more informed global citizens. Finally, the newsletter is a good way to introduce the program to potential friends that may be able to support various Class initiatives.

VII. Periclean World Corner (PWC)

What is the idea behind the PWC?

The purpose of the PWC is fairly straightforward: the intent is to create and sustain a revenue stream for the Periclean Scholars program at Elon University. Periclean Scholars (and Mentors) bring back goods from their travels (i.e.: scarves from India) and these items are then sold at the PWC. The revenue will then go to the Periclean Scholars Alumni Association or to current Classes.

What about import laws?

At this point we are operating at such a minor level with single students, bringing back relatively small amounts of goods (value of approximately $100.00), and in the present case we are beneath the level of official concern regarding import laws. However, the owner of the store where the PWC is located is working on getting his import credentials certified such that in the future he will become the import agent. Details on how that will work are still being determined.

Where is this PWC?

The PWC is a small, clearly marked and branded space in a retail outlet called "For Every Season" inside the Holly Hill Mall on Huffman Mill Road in Burlington, NC. The store has a good, central location in the mall with reasonable traffic.

Who owns "For Every Season?"

David Higham, Periclean Scholars Class of 2006, owns and operates this store (as well as many other businesses in the local area) and it has been in business since 2010.

How long has this initiative been active?

The PWC was put into place just before Christmas in December 2011.

What kinds of items can be put up for sale?

The general rule of thumb is that anything that will sell can be put on display at the PWC, but that is the catch: what will sell can be very tricky to predict. The safest route to go, at least in this beginning stage of the operation, is to think in terms of reasonably priced gift items ($1.00-$30.00) that one might buy as a small gift for a family member or friend. Single items are discouraged in favor of 10+ of the same item. Also, items that are smaller and/or easier to display are preferred.

Can these items also be bought online?

David is working on getting more of these items for sale online, but at this point there is a bottleneck in terms of having the time and resources maximize the potential of this retail outlet opportunity.

Is there information about what country these items come from at the PWC?

One goal of this project is to help educate buyers about fair trade items and grassroots fundraising efforts. To every extent possible, item on display at the PWC should have information about the origin of the item with details about the people who made it and the way in which these people are benefiting from the sale of these items.

Can you give me an example?

Yes. In January 2014, Dr. Arcaro traveled to the University of Monterrey and, while there, bought $100.00 worth of handmade diaries from the Kimakul retail outlet on campus. This is from the Kimakul site: "Kimakul is an organization that seeks to assist low-income people in the development of products for personal and commercial purposes. The word "Kimakul" means "with joy from the heart." For Every Season now has these items and is selling them at a 100% markup, thus potentially generating $100.00 for the Periclean program as well as supporting a wonderful cause in Mexico. A flyer with information about Kimakul is near the items now for sale at the PWC.

How can Periclean Scholars become more directly involved in this operation?

David would love to have business interns working on the project on a regular basis and well as students with skills in online marketing. In a more general way, students can be involved in helping to publicize and market the PWC using social media, word of mouth, and other ways of spreading the word.

What percentage of profits goes to David Higham and "For Every Season?"

David is absorbing all overhead costs for this operation. He is taking 20% of the profit of all items for his business. This percentage may vary over time. This partnership must be and be seen as a "win-win" for all parties. The agreement is that David will write a check to the Periclean Scholars every month with the amount based on sales.

What is the long-term plan for this endeavor?

The plan at this point is to grow the operation and have a modest, steady revenue stream. The relationship with For Every Season and David will be assessed on a regular basis (at least every six months).

VIII. Periclean Graduation Sashes

Where were the first sashes made?

The idea of having sashes made for the graduating Class was conceived by a few 2010's and a 2011 that was in Ghana for the semester. A design and instructions were sent to a contact in Ghana who then located some local artisans who could weave a kinte-cloth like sash with the Periclean logo, the logo for the Class of 2010 and "Periclean Scholars" woven into the material. The sashes were couriered back to Elon by an Elon student  just days before graduation. Neither the Mentor, Dr. Heidi Frontani nor most of the 2010's knew about the sashes until the evening of their graduation dinner with classmates and their families.

How were the first sashes presented?

As part of the dinner celebration program each 2010 was called forward and their Mentor placed the sash around their neck, providing a material representation of the completion of the undergraduate phase of the student's journey as a Periclean Scholar.

What are the stories of the Classes of 2011, 2013 and 2014?

The Class of 2011 worked with a batik artisan in Kandy, Sri Lanka who handmade each sash. A sample remains on display in Kandy in the artisan's shop. The 2012's had their made by women and girls at the Comprehensive Rural Health Project in Jamkhed, India from remnant of saris. Each sash has the same design but each has a different color and pattern of cloth. The 2013's had theirs designed and made in a very

small village in southern Chiapas, Mexico, the village that they visited as seniors. The 2014's had theirs designed and produced by their partners in West Virginia. Partners of the 2015's are producing the sashes for the Class of 2015 in Haiti.

Does anyone else get a sash other than the graduating Pericleans?

Yes. The Mentor, the Director and President Lambert are typically provided with a sash and one is reserved for display purposes. As a side note, for several years Dr. Lambert kept on display in his office at the Maynard House the 2010 sash.

Who pays for the sashes?

The sashes are made by artisans in the country or region of focus and are paid for through funds raised by the Class or from the general Periclean account. In past years the sashes have been made for between $5.00 and $10.00 per sash. Using local artisans is an additional pathway to deepening the ties between the Pericleans and their local partners.

Who designs the sashes?

Design for the sashes has typically been a joint effort between the Class and the local artisan who is provided with dimensions and logo images. As with all decisions regarding the sash, who is contacted to produce the sashes and how they are designed is a Class decision.

How long in advance should a Class begin planning for their sash?

Given all of the factors that must be taken into account to get the sashes in time for graduation, planning must take place at least several months in advance. More recent Classes have begun planning as soon as their junior year. Planning and delivery factors include (1) deciding to participate in the tradition of having a sash, (2) deciding how design will be determined (i.e., Class design or design of local partner(s)), (3) the time it takes to actually produce the sashes, and (4) the time it takes to get the sashes from the local artisan to the Class.

What is the future plans for this tradition?

The expectation is that every Class will want to have some representation of their Periclean commitment displayed on their graduation gown and sashes have now been a tradition since 2010.

Where are past sashes displayed?

Sashes are permanently displayed in the Periclean Scholars meeting space, Global Commons 202, that one day will be filled with colorful reminders of each Classes country or region of focus.

VX. Periclean 5K Fundraiser

Welcome to the Periclean 5K manual! This race was started in an effort to combat hunger in the local community. Our hope with this manual is that it will provide everything you need in order to successfully plan the Periclean 5K each spring. In it you will find tips on how to prepare ahead of time and run race day logistics, order t-shirts, get donations from corporate sponsors, advertise both to Elon and the Burlington community, and individuals to communicate with on campus. Our hope is that you update the manual every year and then pass it down to the next grade. Good luck with planning and have fun! Following the timeline and being proactive should ensure a successful event.

Sincerely,
Sarah Oldham, Brittany Garrett, and Sarah Oldham
Periclean Scholars 2012

Timeline

Planning the Periclean 5K can be time-consuming given the scope of the logistics, community outreach, and advertising necessary to make the event a success. Having a dedicated committee and well-organized plan will go a long way in streamlining the process. Based on our experiences, we've compiled the following month-by-month timeline. These are, of course, suggestions – feel free to adapt our guidelines to make them work for your class. Just remember – the earlier you start planning, the better! We can't emphasize this enough.

September

- Form a class committee. While the entire class should be supportive and informed throughout the planning process, it's most efficient to divide tasks among a group of three to five committed individuals.
- Set a date. If you haven't done so already, it's important to do this *now*. Field-based events fill up very quickly on Elon's campus, so to secure the necessary locations and approvals in time for the event, you want to have a date picked as soon as possible. It would be wise to pick a back-up date, too – one you could reserve as a rain date in the event you had to make last-minute changes. (A Student Life fundraising event, for example, forced our 2012 class to change the date and lose space reservations last-minute.)
- Register the event. Use Elon's SPACES system to register the event on the fields you need. We recommend starting and

ending the route at Elon's intramural fields by Holt Chapel.
- Secure necessary approvals. This will slow you down if you wait, so get in touch with contacts like Moseley Center, Campus Rec, and Campus Security sooner rather than later.
- Work with Elon Volunteers! Collaborate with EV! early on to discuss how both organizations can best share responsibilities for race-planning.

October

Set fundraising goals. Consider:
- How much do you want to earn for your class sustainability efforts? Remember that profits will be split evenly with EV!
- How much do you want to charge per participant? How many runners do you need to meet your goal?
- How much money do you want to secure from donors?
- Reach out to donors. Compile a list of businesses to contact, then organize dates for letter-writing, phone calls, and in-person visits to tell potential donors about the event. *Note: this is time-consuming, but crucial in order to make the event a successful fundraiser to support your Periclean class efforts. Plan on devoting a good chunk of your fall to recruiting donors.*
- Follow up with donors.

November

- Continue reaching out to donors.
- Prepare posters, etc. for advertising. Once spring semester arrives, it'll go quickly. You'll do yourself a huge favor if you have advertisements at least mocked up by the end of fall semester.
- Start the website. It doesn't have to go live yet, but as mentioned above, spring semester will be much smoother if you already have something to work with coming back from winter term.

February

- Follow up with donors. Secure more if needed!
- Finalize advertisements. These should cover both on- and off-campus promotions
- Finalize website.
- Finalize t-shirt design and place orders.
- Set up online registration. You can contact 2012 Periclean Scholars Class-mentor Martin Kamela for more information about how to do so.
- Begin promotions in the local community. Reach out to school track and cross country teams, local running clubs, health clubs, etc.

March

- Distribute posters at Elon and in Burlington.
- Recruit participants from Periclean and EV! Issue challenges to promote maximum involvement from the hosting organizations.
- Reach out to other Elon organizations.
- Launch website and online registration.
- Arrange to have the *Pendulum* cover the event.

April

- Continue advertising!!
- Take care of pre-race and race day logistics. This includes race bibs, sign-in tables, and marking the route.
- Make final contact with donors. If you have food and prize donations, make arrangements to pick these up.
- Contact Physical Plant and Environmental Services. Follow up with Campus Security. You'll need to make sure to have trash cans, tables, bathroom access, and an officer present at the event.

May

- Send thank you cards to donors. Keep your relationships

strong – they may want to sign on for next year!

- Promote the event's success. Write about the event for the Periclean Scholars newsletter and other media.
- Update this manual. Make note of new contacts and strategies for next year's class before sending it along to the appropriate people.

Community Partnerships - Donations

When we started this race in 2011, the idea was to have a community partner in order to bring together Elon students and the greater Burlington community. Taylor Blackburn, the senior in charge of the inaugural race, reached out to Brenda Allen at the former food pantry in Burlington, and the two of them partnered to co-host the race. Unfortunately, in the second year, this partnership fell through. For this reason, we decided to partner with Elon Volunteers! on campus, which you will find out more about in that section. Despite this change in co-sponsoring the event, you will still want to have that community involvement because that's really what the race is about. You can request donations from the community, either monetary or product, and this can be a great way to tie the university and local area together.

Letter to Potential Donors

You can reach out to potential donors by sending them a letter that briefly details what the event is about, where the funds are going and why it's important that they make a donation. You will find a sample letter in the appendix of this manual. Some details that you want to be sure to include: details of the event along with web address, information about co-sponsors, where the proceeds are going, what is required of the organization donating, and how the organization will be recognized. If you start planning early enough (and we highly recommend starting early!), you can have sponsor names somewhere on the t-shirt. You should also be putting names on any banners you print for the event, and on your website.

Types of Donations

What should you ask for as far as a donation? Like we said, it can simply be money. In our case this year, we were unsuccessful in getting anyone to donate money. However, several companies that we contacted were interested in donating gift cards or small products. These can be great to use as prizes for times, most creative way of carrying cans, or as raffle prizes. You will also want to consider asking restaurants and/or grocery stores for food donations. You will need to provide food and beverages on the day of the race. Often, grocery stores are unable to donate if they are a chain because they have national headquarters to report to, and they are unable to give donations from individual stores. However, you can reach out to local restaurants, or even possibly the Company Shops market in downtown. You can also ask companies to help you pay for t-shirts for the race, which can be a very expensive part of the event. You will find more information about t-shirts in that respective section.

Donation Form

_____ will be sponsoring the second annual 5K Bread Bolt, hosted by Elon University's Periclean Scholars, in the amount of $_____.

Please enclose this form with a check in the amount noted above, specifying "5K" in the memo line, in the envelope provided. You will receive a note confirming your contribution to the event. Thank you for donating!

Following Up

In addition to sending this letter, you will need to follow up with the organizations. This can be done by calling the organizations about one week after you have delivered the letters. We recommend delivering them in person, rather than in the mail. You are much more likely to give the letter to the right person if you can do this. If you follow up with a phone call, be prepared. Cold calling is a daunting task, but if you do this with a few people, it gets easier as you go along. Additionally, if you hand-delivered the letter and have someone specific to ask for, you will not be as intimidated when asking to speak with that person on the phone.

Example Letter

On behalf of the Periclean Scholars program at Elon University, we are asking for your support in our second annual 5K Bread Bolt, a spring fundraising event to support charitable projects both in the local community and abroad. Given your role as a respected and influential business in the area, we are asking for your support in the preferred amount of a $100 donation to support this community cause. The event will take place on Elon University's campus on April 21, 2012 and will attract a wide range of participants, including runners from the university and local community. All proceeds raised will go toward Elon University's Periclean Scholars and the projects the program supports. In addition to the monetary registration fee, participants will be asked to bring three canned goods to the event and, tapping into their creative talents, carry the cans around the course to three drop-off locations. The cans will then be donated to a local food bank to help end hunger in Alamance County.

An Elon University organization, Periclean Scholars is a civic engagement program composed of four classes working on development initiatives with local and international partners. Currently, classes are working on issues including rural health and women's empowerment in India, poverty and women's issues in Mexico and rural development in Appalachia. Proceeds generated by the Periclean Scholars program will contribute to the sustainability of these ongoing projects worldwide, as well as to support local partnerships with organizations including the Burlington Housing Authority and Hillcrest Elementary School.

Please consider how your donation will be a meaningful contribution to the success of this fundraising event, and the impact you will be making on our local community. Last year, this event attracted more than 75 runners, resulting in more than 225 canned food donations. This year, we are setting our fundraising goal at $5,000 and plan to double participation to 150, thus donating at least 450 cans. Monetary donations in the form of checks can be made out to Periclean Scholars with an indication in the memo line specifying "5K". Thank you in advance for your contribution. We look forward to hearing from you. Please feel free to contact us via email or phone with any comments, questions or concerns.

Sincerely,
Brittany Garrett   Tom Arcaro
Class of 2012   Director of Periclean Scholars

On-Campus Promotions

As we all know, Elon tends to be a pretty over-programmed campus –
meaning that in order to attract participation, you're going to have to
reach out to students, faculty, and staff in as many ways as possible.
Here are some ideas.

Participation in Periclean Scholars and EV!

- Encourage all Pericleans to participate in the race! Ask Dr.
  Arcaro to send an email to all of the Periclean Scholars,
  challenging them to not only run the race themselves but to
  also recruit at least one friend outside the organization to run
  it with them. We think a prize might be a fun incentive –
  something like a breakfast for the class with the most
  participation.
- EV! programs should also be encouraged to participate in the
  race! While specific challenges to recruit EV! participants
  will ultimately fall under an individuals responsibilities, we
  had an idea to issue a similar competition-based challenge –
  something like an ice cream social for the EV! program with
  the highest percentage of involvement.

Connecting to Other Organizations

- Use campus media to promote the race! Reach out to the
  Pendulum to get coverage before and during the race. Contact
  WSOE and Phoenix 14 News. Send targeted emails to other
  Elon organizations, including Running Club, intramural
  sports, and Greek Life.
- Reach out to faculty and staff, too! Have everyone in your
  class talk to their professors and respective department heads.
  Encourage participation from staff you know.

General Advertising

- Posters! Just make sure to get them approved at the Moseley front desk – simply drop off a copy and fill out a flyer approval form. They'll stamp it and return it to you in a day or two – make copies of this one to distribute on campus.
- Digital ads! You can find the template and instructions for digital board posters on the Moseley Campus Center page of Elon's website.
- Moseley tables! The first week of major advertising on campus, run Moseley tables. Have computers set up so that students can register on the spot. Get Phoenix cash swipers so students can pay that way, too. Accept early canned donations.
- Chalking! This also needs to be approved at the Moseley front desk – just ask for a form.
- Table tents! Contact Aramark to advertise this way in all of the campus dining halls.
- WORD OF MOUTH. When it comes down to it, this is the most effective way of recruiting participants. Tell your friends, your neighbors, your professors. Make sure this isn't just a committee effort – everyone in your class should be actively promoting the race.

Off-Campus Advertising/Promotions

As Elon students, we tend to think strictly about the audience we have right here on campus. One way we hope this event is unique, is that it brings together both members of the Elon University community and members of the Burlington community and beyond. By doing this, you will continue to foster relations between the school and the town, and increase the funds you are able to raise.

Here are some ideas of how to advertise to members of the outside community:

- Reach out to high schools track teams in the area. This is something we thought of but never did. Try to contact the coaches and see if they can make it a mandatory community service event for the team. (Western Alamance, Williams, etc.)

- Reach out to health clubs in the area. You can put flyers in gyms and have them spread the world in general.
- Put up flyers in places like the church Allied Churches is a part of, the Co-op, the Eddy in Saxapahaw, The Root- places where 'running types' may go.
- Go on the local Burlington radio and advertise!

Pre-Race and Race Day Logistics

Website

You will want to create a website for the event. If you are able to buy a domain name, we recommend doing so. If you are not skilled at HTML or coding, you can buy this through Wordpress, and you will be able to update the site as if it were a blog. This may be something that is done in future years, depending on how profitable the event is, because you will need to pay for the domain and for use of the theme. This is something that needs to be worked into the budget. If you want to start out using a generic Wordpress account, though, you can easily set one up. If you can create one using a Periclean email account, that would be best so it can be easily passed along to future classes.

Some things you definitely want to include on your website:
- Date, time, location
- Link to online registration
- Price (early and day-of)
- About the organizers
- Where the proceeds are going
- Why the race is being hosted
- Community sponsors/donors
- Contact information

Online Registration

We highly recommend having online registration as an pre-race day option. Not only does this make things a lot easier in terms of staffing people day-of, you will also have a good idea of how many t-shirts you might need, bib numbers, food, etc. You can use Elon's system for online registration. Talk with your Mentor about setting this up. You can also contact the 2012 Mentor, Martin Kamela, about how to set it up (mkamela@elon.edu). While the 2012 seniors started an online registration, we did not have it operating live, so our experience is somewhat limited in terms of setting it live and then using that information to determine who would be attending the race. One nice thing about having online registration through Elon is that it is free and you can have racers pay online through Elon's payment system. If you decide to use a site such as Active.com, you will have to pay an initial fee, as well as a fee per racer that signs up. We strongly recommend using this system that is already in place through Elon. Just be sure to post the link to registration on your website so people can easily access it.

On-Site Registration

You can also have on-site registration for people who show up the day of the race. We had decided we would charge $5 more for day-of registration, and it could only be cash. We also had the stipulation that the first 100 registrants would be the only runners who would receive a t-shirt. This combination created an incentive for people to sign up ahead of time, which is helpful for you because it makes the registration table less hectic on the day of the event. For both this registration and that which is online, you will likely need a statement saying that the runner will not hold Elon, Periclean Scholars, or any other partner liable in case of emergency. We did not have to deal with this, but you will want to seriously consider this. You can speak with Campus Security for more details on what you may need to include. By completing the online registration, they will be complying with this statement. You may want to have registrants sign a form for this as well. And don't forget, you will need to have another line for parents/guardians of minors, if there is anyone under the age of 18 who may be running.

Parking

How many people are you expecting to show up at the event? Be sure that there is adequate parking at whatever location you are hosting the race. You can find more information about the route and starting location in a later section.

Registration Table

At the registration table, you will want to have different lines. You'll need signs to designate which line is for which purpose. For example, you'll want one that is specifically for people registering for the first time. You'll want another line for those who are just checking in. You will need to have the bibs available at the location where people check in. It may be helpful to have the runner names written on the bib, but you can also write it on when you hand out the numbers.

Race Bibs

Even though the primary objective of this race is not to have the best time, you will still need to provide bib numbers for all runners. Campus Rec uses http://www.runningcount.com/ to get bibs for the Turkey Trot in the fall. There are different options for customizing the bibs. Be sure to buy enough for at least one year. If, for example, you order numbers 1-1000 (just to have enough for a few years, at least), tell the upcoming seniors to order number 1001-2000 so that there are not any duplicates from year to year. You will also need to provide safety pins for the runners to attach them to their shirts.

Race Route & Other Necessities

As long as there are not other events happening on the weekend that you would like to have the event, this would be the best option for you. You will need to check with Peter immediately after picking a date to verify that your event can be hosted on that date. If you wait, there may be other events scheduled in the spring, and you will be out of luck. If you can schedule the event starting in the fall semester, you will have priority over other intramural or club sports because those games are generally not scheduled at that point. However, also keep in mind that Festivus could interfere with your date. If you have any connections with the host that year, use them!

If you need to use a different route besides the one used for Turkey Trot, you will need to pass this by Campus Security if it is on-campus and/or Elon Police if it is on Elon roads. Do this early on as well so that you know you have an established route. You will want to have the police on your side when you are running the race so they can help with safety of runners. If you have this alternative route, you will need to ensure that it is the appropriate length. You can reach out to the running coaches (cross country or track) to see if they have a marker that you can borrow. Neither Campus Rec nor Campus Security have one in their possession right now. You may also need to contact Campus Security and/or Physical Plant about the opening of a building in order to use restrooms. If this is not possible, you will need to provide PortaPotties for runners.

Finish Line

At the finish line, you will need to have approximately 4-5 volunteers recording times of runners. The easiest way to do this is to have people designated to hold timers and to have others writing down times according to bib numbers. This will take some coordination, but it can be done. If you reach out to students who are working with the Turkey Trot, they will likely be able to give you more advice on how this process can work efficiently.

8. Sustainability

❖

A component of any successful organization is to continue growth as a program during undergraduate years and post graduation. The recruitment process is a crucial part in promoting success for the future, and tips for both applicants and Mentors are included below. Additionally, Periclean Foundation was created to ensure long-term sustainability after a Class's time spent together at Elon. The Periclean Foundation allows for a continued communication among alumni regarding their passion for the work they have done, and are now doing, post graduation.

Future Classes: Application Process

Each Class of Periclean Scholars typically contains about 30 students on average and strives to combine a variety of majors and interests. Requirements and components for applying are determined by the current Mentor. In the past, the application required a cumulative GPA of 3.0, a short biographical essay, a letter of recommendation from COR 110 instructor, and an interview with the Class Mentor.

The interview process should help the student to understand the time commitment demanded by the Periclean Scholars' program.

You might consider bringing a sign-up sheet for interviews to each pod presentation. A 10-15 minute interview should suffice, especially if you provide a lot of information about program requirements in a brochure and/or presentation at the pod. Some students will not have participated in a COR 110 pod and may need a bit more of your time. We have noticed that if you have sign-up sheets for appointments within a day or two of a pod that almost everyone who signs up shows up. If you have students sign up for interview appointments weeks after a pod, the chances of them showing up are greatly diminished.

Recruitment Tips for Mentors

During the second half of the fall semester and the first half of the spring semester, the Mentor for the incoming Class and current Pericleans will be giving a series of presentations regarding the Periclean Scholars Program to current first year students currently enrolled in COR 110 classes. These are called PODS.

It is important to begin organizing these PODS early, as it will take a lot of time to coordinate with Global professors who may begin planning their syllabus during the summer.

When conducting interviews, here are some questions to consider:

- How did you learn about our program?
- Why are you interested in being a Periclean Scholar?
- What questions, if any, do you have about the program?
- What is your proposed major? What is your proposed minor, if any?
- What extracurricular activities, if any, do you engage in on campus? (Are you a member of an athletics team, planning to join, or member of any other specialized program such as Honors, Fellows, a Sorority, etc. that might compete for your time?)
- If accepted into the program, what would you hope to accomplish as a Periclean?
- What do you see yourself potentially doing after graduating from Elon?

- What relevant skills do you see yourself potentially bringing to the program? (Have you engaged in service learning, fundraising, written longer research papers, etc.?)
- Do you have plans to study abroad? Where and for how long?
- Any other questions, comments, and things you'd like to share?
- Get as much information about the students as possible
- When you are selecting students for your Class, give some consideration to diversity of majors, backgrounds, and skill sets. It will be desirable to have a Class that includes a 'natural' webmaster, accountant, group of fundraisers, researchers to give SURF and NCUR presentations, writers for the Pendulum, Colonnades, documentarians, etc.

Application components and deadline

Traditionally, the applications for Periclean Scholars have been due the Friday before Spring Break. Normally the students are asked to write a short biographical essay and obtain a letter of recommendation from their COR 110 or other relevant instructor for the application. In 2007, to enhance academic rigor, a short research essay component was added to the application process and the minimum GPA was raised from 2.5 to 3.0. This has since changed, and now the Mentor can choose whether or not they will use a students GPA as a prominent factor in the application process. The Faculty Mentor may choose to read the application essays and make decisions on his or her own or to invite other Mentors or even students to be part of the application review process.

Ask students to include a header on their application with their name, campus box (to facilitate sending out letters), major, GPA, etc.

Be flexible

You recruit your Class to do work in a particular country or region (such as the 2014's in Appalachia). Have a backup plan for whatever you or the students wind up choosing to be the Class' focal topic. If the country or region selected suddenly goes to war or has a coup, how will you proceed? Having thought about some possible alternatives in advance might prove helpful in such a case. To date, the 2008's were unable to visit the school they were helping to construct in Chiapas, Mexico because of security issues (localized infighting among the Zapatistas) and went to another school instead. The 2009's had to change their country of study from Angola to Zambia due to security issues (landmines) and language issues (they speak Portuguese in Angola). Finally, the Class of 2011 was unable to travel to Sri Lanka over Winter Term because of unrest (bombings related to the Tamil separatist movement).

As Mentor, you should think of the Class as a small non-governmental organization. As with any NGO, you will want to recruit people with a range of skills, from fundraising to media production, researching, event planning, and speech giving. Make use of experts who have experience working with or running NGOs (Elon's Business School, EV!, Service Learning, etc.). Mentoring a Periclean Class will require a wide variety of skills such as flexibility, dedication, knowledge, and understanding. A Class of Periclean Scholars should contain a wide variety of majors, interests, backgrounds, and skills in order to create the best possible project and experience.

For a Sample Application Form, see chapter 9.

Tips to Mentors in Facilitating Project Selection

Each specific Class creates a survey in order to assess the future of each individual project. The survey can be as detailed as the class wants it to be. For an example survey, see Chapter 9.

Post Graduation

Periclean Scholars Alumni Association (PSAA)

Upon graduation, you become a member of the Periclean Scholar Alumni Association (PSAA). You can consider taking part in the opportunity to undergo a two-tier term as your Class representative on the Steering Committee of the PSAA. Though your Class is no longer meeting regularly, it is important to stay in communication with your Classmates and your Mentor using all appropriate social networking vehicles. Also, continue to maintain contact with the organizations with which your Class partnered, and especially the individuals that your Class invited to campus as Pericleans-in-Residence. Keep in communication with the Elon University Alumni Relations office and be aware of travel opportunities back to your country/region of focus. Donate regularly to Elon University and designate your gift to go directly to Project Pericles knowing that these funds will go directly to the PSAA and will directly benefit the partners that Classes have vetted. Find out if the organization or business that you work in has a philanthropic outreach office and find out how this entity might be a resource for the PSAA. Also, find out if the organization or business that you work for has a matching program for donations. Be sure to keep up with the Periclean Blog and consider forwarding it on to family, friends, and work associates. Always remember the reason you made the commitment to become a Periclean Scholar as a first year student at Elon. Never let that passion wane because it is you at your best and, more importantly, you continuing to make a difference in our world as a true global citizen.

Through the Redwoods Group Endowment Fund for the Sustainment of the Periclean Scholars Program, the mission chosen by each Class can be sustained in perpetuity. The word 'sustainability' runs throughout conversations among all Periclean Scholars Classes and is the key litmus test for any project. Each cohort of the Periclean Scholars grapples with that question, as the students craft their own mission statement and work toward their long-term service learning project. The inaugural Class of Periclean Scholars established the Periclean Scholars Alumni Association with the vision that Periclean Scholars would make their involvement to their cause life long by staying in contact with each other and coordinating their long-term efforts.

Under the direct mentorship of and with counsel from the Director of Project Pericles, the Periclean Scholars Alumni Association will gather every year with the charge of examining proposals from past and current Periclean Scholars Classes (or, more specifically, the non-government organizations with whom they partnered, e.g., Schools for Chiapas or Catholic AIDS Action). The group makes recommendations on a distribution of funds from the Redwoods Fund. With guidance from Elon faculty and the Redwoods Group, the alumni would evaluate each past project and make a decision on how best to invest the proceeds from the Redwoods Group Endowment

Fund. Evaluation and reporting will be central to the work of this group with annual activity reports sent to Redwoods Group.

Alumni will be asked to contribute to the fund over time in order to increase its impact. With funds from alumni and the Redwoods Group, the amount of the endowment will increase, and new members of the Periclean Scholars program would begin their mission knowing that whatever they choose to pursue will live on far past their undergraduate years.

The objective here is twofold. The primary goal is to make the projects initiated by each Class more sustainable. A second but critical goal is to make the entire Periclean Scholars program even more vibrant and sustainable by giving alumni a lifelong home for their outreach passions.

In order for the association of Redwoods Group and Periclean Scholars to be most meaningful, the Redwoods Group leadership or others from the organization may be in contact with the Elon students as they plan their projects and travel. The Redwoods Group CEO will be available to speak to the students in the program regarding the responsibility of a corporation to improve the global human condition. Finally, Redwoods Group would hold open some spots in their summer Undergraduate Leadership Program for Periclean Scholars who are rising seniors.

A gift of $125,000, payable over five years, will provide both an endowed fund at the end of the pledge period ($100,000) and a restricted annual gift ($5,000 per year). This will mimic the future endowment payout and allow the funds for Periclean Scholars to be available immediately. Other gifts may be added, including those of Periclean Scholars alumni themselves, to expand the endowment in the future.

Important update on the above information:

The Class of 2012 left as one of their legacies the creation of the Periclean Foundation, now a U.S government recognized and registered 501c3. At this writing, a website for the Periclean Foundation and banking technicalities are being worked on. As per the advice of alumni who met at homecoming in 2014, the Periclean Foundation will be the successor to the Periclean Scholar Alumni Association, and in all future discussions, we will be referring to the Periclean Foundation.

Alumni Survey

In December 2012, I [Dr. Tom Arcaro] sent out an email with a request to fill out a survey regarding the long-term impact of being a Periclean Scholar. Out of 153 alumni, we received 81 responses for a total response rate of 52.9%. Here is a breakdown of the response rate per class: Class of 2006 — 44.8%; Class of 2007 — 40%; Class of 2008 — 53.3%; Class of 2009 — 66.6%; Class of 2010 — 53%; Class of 2011– 43.3%; Class of 2012– 72%. The purpose of the survey was to look at the long-term impact that being a Periclean Scholar has after graduation. Below are some highlights of the data.

86% of alumni responded that being a Periclean Scholar had a major or moderate impact on their career path, with only 13.6% saying that the program had little to no impact. In the same way, 95% of alumni said that being a Periclean Scholar had some, or a great deal, of

influence on their non-career life choices. One alumnus commented, "Periclean Scholars has been my most life-changing experience so far, hands down. Through Periclean Scholars, I  traveled outside the US for the first time, found direction in my career path, honed my skills and passions, and worked with an incredible, inspiring group of colleagues I'm proud to count among my closest friends." Another wrote, "Periclean helped me in terms of having experience. I now work for one of the world's largest development organizations (World Vision), working with college students. Having experience doing development work as a college student really helped me get in the door and has also helped me as I think about our audience. Why do these students care? Why should they care? What kinds of stories would they want to hear? Issues and people they would be interested in? Etc. My Periclean Scholars experience has been incredibly valuable in this job."

The survey also focused on individual's current knowledge of their Class' project and county of focus. When Alumni were asked about the extent to which they have kept up with news and events related to their Class' county of focus, 74% said they have kept up somewhat, with 13.6% closely keeping up. 12% of alumni have kept up very little with their Class' country of focus. One respondent wrote, "While I do try to stay up to date on what is going on in India (I follow the Times of India on Twitter), it has become harder since there is so much going on in my own community that I want to be aware of. Still trying to find a balance." More alumni have kept up with their Class' issue of focus in their community with 59% somewhat keeping up and 24.7% closely keeping up.

The survey asked whether travel to the Class' county of focus had occurred and nine alumni had said that they had been on an average of two trips.

The Periclean Scholars program requires contact among Class members, Mentors, and the Director. The survey asked how often the individuals have maintained contact with members of their Periclean Class and the majority responded that they had occasional or frequent contact with fellow members of their Class. Only ten responded that they have had very little contact with members in their Class.

The Director keeps in contact through regular emails and a newsletter update, on average every six weeks. In the survey Alumni were asked how thoroughly they read the newsletter. 40.7% said they read it thoroughly, 7.4% pass it on to others after reading, and the rest of the respondents said they glance through the newsletter.

The majority of individuals described contact with the Director as a moderate level of contact, although the level of contact with their

Class Mentor was significantly less with 32 responders saying they have had very little contact with their Mentor and 35 responders saying they have had a moderate level of contact. Only 11 individuals have maintained close contact.

When asked how their Mentor can better serve individuals' needs, one comment read, "I think it would be great for each Mentor to set up either a conference call or a video chat type forum that once per year or so, the whole class can be invited to call in to briefly update each other on their lives and their class project."

We also asked about a series of questions regarding finances and knowledge of the Periclean Scholar Alumni Association and Periclean Foundation. Only 12 responders were not aware that there was an Alumni Association or Periclean Foundation. The majority of responders were aware of the Association and Foundation but only had a vague idea of how it works.

When asked how the Association can better serve, one comment read, "Finding some way to bridge the gaps of distance between students would be good. The newsletters definitely help because they let Alum know what's going on but as everyone is busy it can feel sometimes like the purpose of reaching out is only to ask for donations/fundraising – which, to be fair, is a factor we committed to when signing on as Scholars – and it can lead to a disconnected feel. I wish I could offer a suggestion as to how to make that easier but I can't think of what could be a good method to ensure people feel engaged on a more dynamic/hands-on level. I would suggest it might be a good idea to look into ways to "reunite" Pericles classes by perhaps organizing service trips during the summer or 1-2 times per year, which alums could go on as well. I know a lot of people from my class continue to travel down to Honduras and I don't know if other classes have people who do the same but I know the interest would be there to continue, "being a Periclean" by doing a service trip even though we've graduated."

When asked about monetary giving, 56 of responders have financially supported the Periclean Scholars Alumni Association or their Class initiatives. 45 of responders have financially supported causes related to their Class' mission.

The survey also asked about what the program was like as an undergraduate. When asked how they would rank Periclean Scholars among the other affinity groups, 49 responses said the Periclean program was more influential in terms of the undergraduate experience compared to other groups. Only 6 individuals said Periclean was less influential than other campus groups. Fellows programs, sororities and fraternities, and sport teams were mentioned among the other groups.

Out of 81 alumni, 58% are currently working, or have obtained a graduate degree. 22.22% are currently working in a formal long-term service program (Teach for America, AmeriCorps, or Peace Corps). 71.6% have participated in a local community service program (Special Olympics, Kiwanis Club, book drives).

Assessing Program Impact

As part of the Elon Periclean Scholars continued plan for growth and academic success, a next step the program hopes to take is the initiative for an external and internal reviewer. Essentially, a qualified professional(s) will visit Elon with the intent of exploring, analyzing and reviewing the different assets of Elon's' Periclean program. This includes the administration, the service work, the social media effort, the efficiency, etc. This will take the program to the next level as it gains acknowledgement and  professionalism. We hope this process will take place in the next year.

Assessing the program's impact on both Elon students and international partners is a top priority this year for many reasons.

- As the program recruits its 13th Class, a comprehensive assessment is long overdue. To this point there is only anecdotal data from various source

- A solid assessment plan is needed in the anticipation of handing the program over to a new director
- Assessment data - both quantitative and qualitative - will be critical as the program seeks additional funding from external and internal sources
- Assessment data is critical in exploring the potential replication of the program. There needs to be a solid model in place as a starting point for other institutional assessments.
- The assessment process will serve to further clarify programmatic goals and objectives
- Assessment of global impact in focus countries (e.g., in the catchment area of the clinic in Kpoeta, Ghana started by the Class of 2010) will attract more external funding and alumni support to the Periclean Foundation

As we discussed currently the assessment plan includes at least the following:

- A re-written alumni survey based on select AACU VALUE rubrics. The tentative long term plan will be to send the survey results bi-annually
- Attain comparison NSSE data going back to the first Class (2006) and initiate a yearly 'automatic' report comparing Periclean and non-Periclean students. Note: It will be important to systematically ensure that the Periclean seniors are aware of the importance of their participation in NSSE
- Explore long term impact on alumni using both targeted interviews of alumni and possible partnership with KCSL on their goal of assessing long term impact
- Begin this year with an annual focus group interview with the graduating senior Periclean Scholars based on select AACU VALUE rubric outcome goals
- Begin this year doing base line assessment of the incoming Class using a focus group method (and compare these data with the results at graduation)
- Begin collecting assessment data of country-of-focus impact. Have each Class develop their own assessment rubrics of their impact before graduation and pass these rubrics on to the Periclean Foundation board members tasked with long term vetting of partners/partnerships

Important update on impact assessment abroad:

At this writing, we have initiated an extensive impact assessment of the partnership between the Class of 2010 and various villages in Ghana. We have also initiated an impact assessment of the partnership between the Class of 2012 and the Comprehensive Rural Health Project (CRHP) in Jamkhed, India. The plan for the next six months, is for there to be similar impact assessments done related to Class initiatives in Sri Lanka, Namibia, Honduras, Zambia, and Mexico (particularly in Chiapas, Mexico).

Key Components for Future Success

I [Dr. Tom Arcaro] have been honored to talk about the Periclean Scholars Program at numerous state, regional, national, and international forums.
Frequently, I was asked "How were you able to create such a program?" In response to these questions and in response to the "Crucible Moment" document, I wrote the comments below describing the history of the program and my vision for possible replication.

A Crucible Moment: College Learning and Democracy's Future

The National Task Force on Civic Learning and Democratic Engagement recently published a study of the nation's Higher Education plans for civic engagement and stressed that the nation's civic health is "anemic" and "concerning." (2012). In previous decades, civic education was often viewed as having knowledge about the different branches of government and United States history. As we move into the 21st century, some educators contend that this basic knowledge is not enough. Learning about democracy in a global context is also critically important and is not currently a part of many curricula within institutions of higher education across the United States. The Task Force writes that, "Democratic knowledge and capabilities are honed through hands-on, face-to-face, active engagement in the midst of differing perspectives about how to address common problems that affect the well-being of the nation and the world" (2012).

The task force sets forth nine components that 21st century civic education should include. These are listed below, followed by how Elon University's Periclean Scholars program addresses each goal/component.

1. **Knowledge of US History, political structures, and core democratic principles and founding documents, and debates-US and global-about their meaning and application.**

Each cohort of Periclean Scholars is encouraged to write letters to their elected officials and to other elected officials relevant to either their local or global initiatives. Additionally, Periclean Scholars annually participate in "Debating for Democracy" organized by the national Project Pericles office. There is a demonstrative emphasis on understanding and owning the role of both local and global citizen.

2. **Knowledge of the political systems that frame constitutional democracies and of political levers for affecting change.**

Periclean Scholars spend extensive time researching their country of focus including the political systems that are both internal and external trans-governmental organizations (e.g., the United Nations) and America's political structures and comparing them. They learn how to reach out to policy makers and government leaders to address social needs and how to facilitate communication and coordination between their partner governing entities.

3. **Knowledge of diverse cultures and religions in the US and around the world.**

A central goal of each Class cohort is to become, effectively, an expert on their nation of focus including countries in the immediate region. This includes researching, reading, and presenting information about the culture, history, politics, economics, geography, religion, current affairs and environment of their country of focus. In order to effectively partner locally they also must understand and be familiar with local cultures as well.

4. Critical inquiry and reasoning capacities.

Periclean Scholars understand that the decisions they must make in regard to creating a Class mission statement are very serious. This mission statement includes topics such as which issue or issues with which to focus, and which partnerships to form. These decisions demand the highest level and most thorough research and must be examined from every possible perspective. When discussing and intervening in social issues worldwide, it is imperative to look at every aspect and angle of an intervention, and the Program encourages that.

5. Deliberation and bridge building across differences.

Participants in the Periclean Scholars program come from all different kinds of backgrounds and majors. The first semester especially, the cohorts of roughly 30 students have to work extremely hard at getting along with each other despite their differences. Agreeing as a Class on important matters such as a Class mission statement, on which issue or issues to focus on, and on which partnerships to form are all tasks that demand critical and effective listening and compromising skills.

6. Collaborative decision-making skills.

Periclean Scholars work as a team to decide the majority of what their Class activities are. These range from the selection of reading assignments and overall syllabus content to deliberating over which partnerships to pursue. The Mentor facilitates and guides these decisions, but the onus is on the students to learn how to most effectively decide nearly all of Class foci and action steps.

7. Open-mindedness and capacity to engage different points of view and cultures.

A major goal of the Periclean Scholars program is to nurture global citizens who learn to always deeply understand the people and cultures with which they work. This commitment can be seen in the Periclean Pledge and is part of the ethos of the program:

8. Civic problem solving skills and experience

In the course of working with both their local and global partners over a period of years, cohorts of Periclean Scholars must deal with a complex variety of local, national and international political bodies. Additionally, they must also navigate the internal civic culture of our university. For example, they must coordinate and collaborate with other entities on campus - both student and administrative - to accomplish goals.

9. Civility, ethical integrity, and mutual respect.

Since Periclean Scholars work together as a cohort for over three years, they learn to work together as a team, respecting each other's personal, as well as, disciplinary perspectives. As junior colleagues to their Mentor and as a body that has extensive contact with institutional, local and international bodies, Periclean Scholars realize that they must always interact as professionals, keeping in mind that they represent not only themselves and their entire Class, but the program and university as a whole.

9. Additional Important Aspects of the Program

❖

The following information can be used as a point of departure for Classes at various stages in the Periclean Scholars Program. Examples of applications, syllabi, etc. from past Classes are included to expedite the processes for future Classes so that they are not "reinventing the wheel." This is not to say that a Class should copy these initiatives verbatim, rather they should discuss them and come up with a plan that works best for their individual Class. Aspects included in this section are as follows:

I.	Sample Application Form
II.	Sample Syllabus
III.	Sample Sustainability Survey
IV.	How to Market Periclean
V.	Vetting Documents
VI.	Example of a Reflective Assignment
VII.	Sample Blog Posts
VIII.	Testimonies from Past Periclean Scholars
IX.	Additional Readings

I.   Sample Application Form

2016 Application for the Periclean Scholars Program
http://www.projectpericles.org/

Name: _____   Campus Box: _____

Major or Intended Major:

_____

First Semester GPA: _____   Email: _____

Global Studies Professor: _____

To be eligible to apply for the Periclean Scholars Program, you must do each of the following:

___ Write a 1-2 page letter of application outlining why you would like to become a Periclean Scholar, what you hope to contribute to the organization, and what you would like to gain from it.

___Write a 1-2 page response to a reading placed on reserve at the library by Professor April Post

___ Complete (or be taking) Global Studies COR 110

___ Submit a letter of recommendation from your Global Studies professor

___ Have a GPA of 3.0 or above

___ Be interviewed by either Dr. Post or Dr. Arcaro before March 1, 2013

___ Complete this application form

All parts of the application are due at April Post' office in Carlton, room 318, by Friday, March 1, 2013, at 4:00 pm.

Background:

Please briefly discuss your four most important or meaningful commitments (organizations, leadership roles, etc.) which you have participated in or are currently participating in.

1.

_____
_____
_____
_____

2.

_____
_____
_____
_____

3.

_____
_____
_____
_____

4.

_____
_____
_____
_____

How did you hear about Periclean Scholars? (Check all that apply)

___ GST 110 Pods ___ Online ___ A Periclean Scholars Event

___ A Professor ___ A current Periclean Scholar ___ Other

(_____)

II.   Sample Syllabi

Below are x number sample syllabi that will give you sense for what can and should be included as each class develops their syllabus every semester. Draft of template syllabus intended as a point of departure for discussion and eventual drafting of a generic syllabus.

GST 225A: Periclean Scholars

Class of 2017
Fall 2014
Dr. Carol A. Smith csmith@elon.edu
Office Hours:
Koury Athletic Center 227 M 12:15-1:15; T 10:30-12:00; W 4:00-5:00
Center for Leadership 101G Th 1:00-4:00

Course information

M/W 1:40-3:20 | Carlton 309
Consult the Moodle website frequently for announcements and course material.
Periclean Scholars Website: http://www.elon.edu/e-web/academics/special_programs/project_pericles/scholars.xhtml
Periclean Scholars Blog: https://blogs.elon.edu/pericleanscholars/
Final Exam Period: Fri. Dec. 5 from 1:00 pm-4:00 Mark your calendar!)

People you should know

- Dr. Tom Arcaro, Elon University Director of Project Pericles and Periclean Scholars Program. arcaro@elon.edu
- Patrick Rudd, Class of 2017 Personal Librarian. prudd@elon.edu
- Catherine Parsons, Program Assistant for the Periclean Scholars Program. cparsons@elon.edu

A note from your Mentor about this course

The purpose of this course: To figure out how we can best use our resources of time, talent and treasure to work towards positive change on an issue chosen by us. It is my responsibility in this first course to help guide you all in the choosing of that issue and begin to figure out how we are going to address it. With that in mind, I have designed the course as follows. I look forward to our next three years together and am excited to see how your passion is going to "inspire global change".

Course Description

(From the Academic Course Catalog) In this foundational course students develop a mission statement for the class and research in depth the issues and topics related to that mission. Emphasis is placed on becoming deeply familiar with the multiplicity of factors that surround the group's chosen issue and developing individual and group goals (short and long term). They examine the process of and begin to understand how to be effective agents of social change. Offered fall semester. Counts toward Civilization or Society requirement.

What you need

- Loeb, Paul Rogat. (2010). Soul of a citizen: Living with conviction in challenging times. NY: St. Martin's Griffin.
- A binder to organize notes and readings, or some way to keep your items together
- Access to our Moodle website

Recommended reading

We will be adding to this list over the years on our library research page with the help of Patrick Rudd, our personal librarian. We will need reference materials, both from a historical perspective as well as current events. I expect that you will provide resources to this list. These resources may be posted to our (2017 Periclean Scholars) Moodle site.
- Lupton, Robert D. (2011). Toxic charity. NY: Harper One.

Goals and objectives

In this course you will...

- Learn about who the members of our cohort are and what skills, experiences and passions they bring to the class
- Learn about the history of the Periclean Scholars program and be able to share that with others both on and off campus
- Learn ways to effectively and efficiently make group decisions and practice using them
- Learn about Namibia and be able to explain historical and political events that have shaped the country and that are currently in progress
- Learn about Namibians and the issues they face.
- Learn about what corporations, groups and organizations are already doing in Namibia
- Learn about what the class of 2006 did in Namibia
- Learn about current social issues in Namibia
- Learn who the important policy makers in the US and Namibia are and examine some of those policies related to the issues being studied
- Evaluate the over-arching issues of helping others
- Examine the process of and begin to understand how to be selective agents of social change
- Evaluate work already being done in Namibia
- Develop a mission statement for the class
- Analyze 8-10 potential projects in Namibia to guide our decision of which project to choose
- Develop individual and class three-year plans and create a roadmap for working on them
- Determine class emphasis for the spring semester

Expectations of students

You are now a member of an elite group of students dedicated to inspiring global change. As such, you are expected to be an engaged collaborator and participant in your learning both in and outside of the classroom and continually reflect and assess your learning in this course. Your learning is dependent upon your commitment level and effort. In this course, you should:

- Demonstrate curiosity, preparation, and participation in a way that furthers your learning and the group's learning
- Make a conscious effort to be a team player. This includes accepting—but addressing—mistakes
- Listen to others' ideas and maintain an open mind even when skeptical
- Be punctual, and attend all class meetings. Attendance has an ethical component: your presence helps the group learn, and your absence hurts the group. You may miss 2 classes without penalty if you are sick or have an emergency. Perfect attendance will earn 1 bonus point on your final grade
- Be involved inside and outside of class. Support fellow Pericleans through participation in Pan-Periclean, committee meetings, and class events
- Seek help when needed
- Demonstrate respect for professor and peers: listen, consider others' opinions and compromise
- Stay abreast of current events in Namibia
- Not be afraid to (a) ask questions; and (b) contribute in class. Adhere to the Full Value Contract and Challenge by Choice philosophies
- Remember that it is not about us ... it is about Namibia and for Namibians
- We commit to taking care of the 2017 Periclean Scholars cohort
- Expect the above from your peers

Expectations of the professor

The professor is the facilitator and Mentor who coordinates the learning connections and maintains the link between the face- to-face exchanges in the classroom and the outside learning spaces and experiences available. I am committed to learning about Namibia and humanitarian aid alongside you and helping you reach your goals. To do my job, I must:

- Make clear my expectations. This includes holding students

accountable to the expectations listed above
- Provide clear explanations of assignments, graded work, and evaluation criteria
- Provide prompt feedback on student work
- Solicit feedback from students on the progress and conduct of the course
- Be accessible
- Treat students fairly and with respect. This extends to evaluating work and assigning grades. I am grading your work, not you
- Provide substantive, compelling, and challenging opportunities for learning and intellectual growth
- Help identify strengths and weaknesses, and devise strategies for improvement
- Make clear why we're doing what we're doing
- Maintain objectivity
- Contribute to the conversations
- Read the class and help facilitate the wellbeing of the class as a whole

Course overview

Note: Phases are meant to be building blocks and practices that should continue throughout the semester. This is not an exhaustive list of what we will be doing, but rather an overview of what types of components you can expect in each phase.

Phase 1: Discovery

- Learn who the members of our cohort are and about their talents, skills, experiences and passions. Related assignments: Life Map/Identity collage. Student-led group activities
- Learn about the Periclean scholars program. Related assignments: Visit by Program Director Dr. Tom Arcaro
- Read the blog and the website
- Learn ways to effectively and efficiently make group decisions and practice using those. Related assignments: Readings posted to Moodle, group discussions, responses to scenarios, and organization of class members into committees

- Learn about Namibia and be able to identify major historical and political events that have shaped the country and that are currently in progress. Keep up with Current Events: Evaluate and present a news item to the class
- Learn about Namibians. Related assignments: Readings found by class members, other sources of information. Identify and learn about what corporations, groups and organizations are already doing in Namibia. Related assignments: develop relationships with contacts we have already: find other contacts

Phase 2: The Issues

- Identify social issues currently at play in Namibia. Related assignments: Continuation of current events: Social issues assignment: Watch documentaries
- Learn who the important policy makers in the US and Namibia are and examine some of the policies related to issues being studied. Related assignments: Investigation of policy makers and the policies they are making
- Evaluate the act of helping others. Related assignments: Reading Toxic Charity or Soul of a Citizen, Articles on Moodle, TBD writing assignment
- Evaluate the work already being done. Related assignments: TBD small group project

Phase 3: Narrowing the Focus

- Write the mission statement for the class and publish it. Related assignments: Research ways to write mission statements. Interview earlier Periclean classes about how they came up with their mission statement. Work together to write the statement
- Analyze 5-6 potential foci of possible projects in Namibia to guide our decision of which project(s) we will choose to focus on. Related assignment: TBD
- Analyze possible potential partners (either local or international). Related assignments: Conversations with potential partners, TBD

Phase 4: Next Steps

Answer these questions:
- Where do we want to be as a class in spring 2017?
- Where do you want to be individually?
  - Related assignments:
    - Class and individual three year plan
- What will be our roadmap for how to get there?
  - Related assignments: TBD
- What will be our emphasis for the spring semester? How can we maintain momentum during break?
  - Related assignments: Class discussion

Course components

Class participation and preparation: (20% of final grade)

Class participation is a major component of this course. Good participation is characterized by focused involvement in individual, small-group, whole-class and Pan-Periclean activities in which you put the well-being of the class first and foremost. Each student is expected to attend class daily, to arrive on time and to remain in the class the entire period. You are also expected to attend the majority of Pan-Periclean events that are held for all of the Periclean classes. Attending class, without contributing comments or pertinent issues and simply responding when called upon will only guarantee you a C-.

Written Work:

- Blog post [1] (5% of grade); each person will, individually or in a small group, write a blog and post to the Periclean Scholars Moodle site (dates already assigned)
- News Forum (15% of grade); each person will, individually, post summary/abstracts of current events (either about Namibian specifically, or Periclean Scholars in general) to the News Forum of the 2017 Periclean Scholars Moodle site. Guidelines: 8 topics; no more than 500 words per response
- Discussion Board (15% of grade); each person will, individually, post responses to current events (either about

Namibian specifically, or Periclean Scholars in general) to the Discussion Board of the 2017 Periclean Scholars Moodle site. The expectation is that you will find 6+ "items" to write about for your primary post. You need to respond to 3+ responses for your secondary posts. Also each person will, individually, respond to questions raised either by myself or a peer, to a discussion board on the 2017 Periclean Scholars Moodle site. This can fulfill secondary posts requirements. The questions can come from a topic from the News Forum, or a reading (such as Toxic Charity, Soul of a Citizen, Letters Left Unsent, etc.) or something that comes up in class
- o Primary posts [6+]
- o Secondary posts [3+]
- o Pose a question [1+]
- Mission Statement (0% of the grade); as a class, develop (at least) the foundation of a mission statement, or (hopefully) the finalized mission statement for the class of 2017
- Reflection Paper (15% of the grade); each person will, individually, write a final reflection paper asking the questions (1) What, (2) So What, and (3) Now What pertaining to the Periclean Scholars Program. The major premise of this reflection is what you have done to progress the process; so what about the importance of the work you have done; and now what are you going to do with the knowledge and information you have gained. Disclaimer: The plan of the reflection paper may change between now and the end of the semester; if so, that will be discussed with the entire class

Mid-term Project/Presentations (15% of the final grade)

- Small group work pertaining to the area of interest (history, geo-political, etc.)

Final Presentation (15% of the final grade)

- Small group work pertaining to potential topic of interest (final project NOT to be determined, but investigating some possible areas to focus upon)
- Grades are an evaluation of the quality of work you've turned

in, not an evaluation of your potential or your intelligence or even how hard you worked, and they certainly are not an evaluation of you as a person

Grades

A grade in the "A" range indicates distinguished performance in a course; virtually flawless, clear, and complex understanding and expression of the material with excellent evidence.

- Completely and whole-heartedly engage in class discussions and activities both in and outside of class through being an active listener and passionate participant
- Make thoughtful contributions to class well-being
- Encourage equal participation and cooperation amongst your peers
- Always have homework and other materials prepared
- Go above and beyond the requirements of the course

A grade in the "B" range indicates a really strong performance, well above-average performance in class.

- Frequently engage in class discussions and activities both in and outside of class through being an active listener and participant
- Make thoughtful contributions
- Most of the time have homework and other materials prepared
- Meet all class requirements

A grade in the "C" range indicates an average performance in which a basic understanding of the subject has been demonstrated; an accurate but average comprehension of the material. The responses answers the questions asked, but fails to elaborate or go into depth or detail.

- Reasonably engage in class discussions and activities through being a good listener and participant
- Make occasional contributions to help meet class goals and objectives
- Sometimes have homework and other materials prepared

- Meet most class requirements

A grade in the "D" range indicates a passing performance despite some deficiencies. An "F" indicates failure to obtain the required score to pass the class.

- Rarely to never engage in class discussions and activities both in and outside of class and fail to participate most of the time
- Rarely make contributions to help meet class goals and objectives
- Monopolize class discussions and decisions
- Rarely have homework and other materials prepared
- Met few class requirements

Grading Scale:
A 93-100 B+ 87-89 A- 90-92 B 83-86 B- 80-82
C+ 77-79 C 73-76 C- 70-72
D+ 67-69 D 63-66 D- 60-62
F 0-59

NOTE: It is YOUR responsibility to check your grades and attendance to verify the information I have entered. Please be sure to check Moodle frequently and let me know immediately if you see any error in your grade and/or attendance.

Academic Message

An Elon student's highest purpose is Academic Citizenship: giving first attention to learning and reflection, developing intellectually, connecting knowledge and experiences and upholding Elon's honor codes. Elon's honor pledge calls for a commitment to Elon's shared values of Honesty, Integrity, Respect and Responsibility. To be clear about what constitutes violations of these values, students should be familiar with the Judicial Affairs policies in the student handbook, including violations outlined at http://www.elon.edu/e-web/students/handbook/violations/default.xhtml. Students with questions about the specific interpretation of these values and violations as they relate to this course should contact this instructor immediately. Violations of the academic-related areas will be documented in an incident report to be maintained in the student's judicial record, and may result in a lowering of the course grade and/or failure of the course with an Honor Code F.

Academic Accommodations for Disabled Students

If you are a student with a documented disability who will require accommodations in this course, please register with Disabilities Services in the Duke Building, Room 108 (278-6500), for assistance in developing a plan to address your academic needs. For more information about academic accommodations, please visit http://www.elon.edu/e- web/academics/advising/ds/.

General policies and procedures

Religious Holidays: In recognition that observance of recognized religious holidays may affect students' classroom attendance and the submission of graded work in courses, Elon University has established procedures for students concerning notifying their instructors of an absence necessitated by the observance. This policy reflects the University's commitment to being responsive to our increasing diversity and to encourage students' spiritual development. Please notify your instructor within the first week of the semester that you will miss class in order to observe a religious holiday. Official notification requires that you complete the Religious Observance Notification Form found at http://www.elon.edu/e-web/students/religious_life/ReligiousHolidays.xhtml. In addition, you must send another notification to your instructor at least one class before each absence and make prior arrangements for completion of any work missed during your absence. All classes missed due to religious holidays will count as one of your two absences allowed during the semester.

Attendance policy: Regular attendance is required; we are learning to work as a team and making critical decisions that will impact the rest of our time together. To allow for illness and other unforeseen circumstances, you are allowed 2 absences. (Three late arrivals and/or early departures constitute one absence.) Every absence over 2, excused or unexcused, will result in your final grade being lowered by 2 points. If you are late to class or cannot come, you are responsible for telling me the reason so it can be documented. Perfect attendance will earn 1 bonus point on the final grade. If you must be absent, please check with a classmate and Moodle so that you make up the work you have missed before the next class. If you need to turn in a missed assignment, you can either send it in with a classmate or drop it off in my office in Koury (Athletic) 227. Work sent via e-mail will "hold your place" but is not accepted as the final product UNLESS the work is specifically requested as an electronic document.

Class Absences Due to Flu-Like Illness: If you are experiencing flu-like symptoms, please do not come to class. You should stay home and self-isolate according to CDC recommendations. Notify me via e-mail as soon as you realize you are ill and cannot attend class. Students who are ill and have flu-like symptoms should consult with Health Services by phone or in person regarding their illness. This will allow for appropriate assessment and treatment and will also create a documentation source for notifying faculty members if a student must self-isolate and miss classes. There are procedures in place for notifying faculty when students are ill and cannot attend class.

E-mail: Be sure to check your e-mail daily in case there are changes in assignments, announcements about events, etc. Teaching classes and attending meetings leaves me time to check e-mail only two or three times a day so please allow me at least 24 hours to respond to any e-mail you send me. I do not have internet access at home; therefore, correspondence will generally take place between 8am and 5pm Monday through Friday.

Moodle: Information pertinent to the course will be posted to Moodle. Please check this site regularly for updated information and assignments.

Elon Writing Center: Elon's Writing Center is staffed by trained peer-consultants who can help you with all of your writing projects (for any class or major and for any extracurricular, personal, or professional purposes), so take advantage of this excellent academic resource and include a visit to our Writing Center as part of your own writing process.

III.   Sample Sustainability Survey

What is important to you in the future and sustainability of our Class' efforts?

For each item please indicate the response which most closely fits your beliefs.

1 = not important 2 = somewhat unimportant 3 = neutral 4 = somewhat important 5 = very important

1. Maintaining contact with community of Kpoeta
2. Maintaining contact with one another as a Class
3. Working together with on-campus Ghana initiatives (fundraising, Friends of Ghana, collaborating with younger 2010 Pericleans, etc.)
4. Maintaining contact with the greater Periclean Scholars Program (younger Classes and alumni from older Classes)
5. Financially supporting the Kpoeta Health Clinic with required monthly/yearly monetary donations
6. Indefinite commitment to health clinic facility maintenance.
7. Pursuing a drug store in the health clinic
8. Expand upon Kpoeta projects in the future (i.e. physician's assistant and midwife for the clinic, road, etc.)
9. Time/financial involvement with initiatives in Sokode (nut shelling machines, Kindergarten, etc.)
10. Time/financial involvement with other Ghana initiatives (book drive, solar cookers, etc.)
11. Supporting one another's personal initiatives/projects that come up post-grad.
12. Having a board of directors (defined responsibilities and positions) for Class members post-graduation
13. Pursuing grants as part of our continued fundraising efforts

Open Ended Questions:

14. How do you envision our Class' role/relationship with Elon University and the greater Periclean Scholars Program post-graduation?

15. How do you envision Dr. Frontani's role post-graduation?
16. What role do you envision for yourself with Periclean Scholars 2010 initiatives post-graduation (donating time, money, etc.)?
17. What are your expectations for the communication of our group post-graduation?
18. What role do you envision for the younger members of our Class (those not graduating this May)?
19. What financial commitment are you willing to make to 2010 projects, if any?
20. What do you think we should call ourselves after graduation?
21. What do you envision would be the role of a potential "board of directors"?
22. How do you envision our fundraising efforts will continue after graduation?

Please write any additional comments/thoughts related to the above.

IV.   How to Market Periclean

On a resume:

Periclean Scholars, Steering Committee Member
April 2013-Present

- Cohort based civic engagement and academic program
- Facilitate 2 classes during the semester, suggest strategies and ideas to classmates to identify, analyze, and assist in vetting possible partner organizations
- Assist in planning 4 fundraising, class relations, or educational events per semester
- Act as a liaison for the Periclean Class of 2016 by maintaining communication between the students and program director

In a cover letter:

Expand upon skills fostered in Periclean, can include:
  1. Critical thinking
a.   Hearing and thinking from different perspectives
b.   Brainstorming sustainability
c.   Understanding how one action can affect many people
  2. Cultural sensitivity
  3. Understanding group dynamics
  4. Being able to maximize potential in the group by getting to know members' strengths and using them
  5. Expressing opinions respectfully

In an interview:

Possible interview questions where you could respond with an example from Periclean:

1. What was the last project you headed up, and what was its outcome?
2. Can you describe a time when your work was criticized?
3. Have you ever been on a team where someone was not pulling their own weight? How did you handle it?
4. Give me an example of a time you did something wrong. How did you handle it?

5. Tell me about a time where you had to deal with conflict on the job.
6. Give examples of ideas you've had or implemented.
7. What's the most important thing you learned in school?
8. What is your greatest achievement outside of work?

V.   Vetting Documents

Partnership Review Questionnaire:

The purpose of this packet is to collect important information on the internal structure and communication, sustainability, finance, and clientele of the partner organization of a class of Periclean Scholars. Each section will ask a series of questions to evaluate the way your organization works, identify it's organizational strengths and areas that could be improved. Your answers to these questions will help the partner class evaluate your organization against our standards for non-profit organizations. This packet has been created from extensive research on sustainability, research on humanitarian aid workers on aspects of effective and harmful non-profit organizations, and the experience of each Periclean Scholars class that has modified it. Please consider the following questions and prepare the requested information for a coming Skype interview that will be conducted by 2-3 members of your partnering class.

General Information

Please discuss the demographics of your target population or partnering communities.

- What led you to that specific population?
- How did you first contact this community? If you actively reach out to other communities, how do you do that?
- What are your points of contact with this population? (leaders/ members you talk to, different parties you communicate with)
- How do you feel they perceive the work you do?
- What needs do you serve in that area?
- Do you have other partners? If so, what is your history with them?
- What projects or programs are currently in progress?
- What has been your most successful project/program?
- What has been your least successful project, and how did the organization learn from it, how did the organization react to it?

Internal Structure and Communication

Please list the members of your board of directors and their specific job descriptions/what they contribute to your organization. Please note if any of them are from or part of your partnering community:

- How often does the board meet, how often does the director communicate with board members?
- What kinds of decisions are made with input from the board, what kinds of decisions does the director make autonomously?
- How often do the leaders in your organization discuss plans for the future?
- How often do the leaders in your organization discuss whether you are meeting your mission?
- Please describe the level of involvement community leaders have in your organizations decision-making process:
- How often is the work of each member of your organization reviewed?
- What other parties do you communicate or interact with? (Local government, partner or other non-profits or organizations, third-party evaluators, financial or resource contributors, etc.)
- What systems are in place to ensure sustainability? How often do you discuss sustainability with your organization's leaders? How is your organization sustainable?
- What training materials or programs are in place to assist the transition from one director (or other organizational leadership positions) to the next?
- How are staff, interns, or new board members or directors trained?
- What are your organization's metrics for measuring impact? (# served, # goods delivered, qualitative feedback, et cetera) In other words, how do you measure your success? How do you know you're doing good and how would you compare the effectiveness of one program or technique versus another?

Finance

- Do you have a current endowment?
- What is your net income?
- How do you raise funds?
- Who are your donors?
- How much of revenue comes from grants, donors, and fundraising events?
- How much time do you spend on efforts, and who is responsible for fundraising?
- What types of fundraising efforts have you made, which were successful and unsuccessful, and why do you think that was?
- Annual costs?
- Are those costs increasing or decreasing?
- Annual revenue, increasing or decreasing?
- Do you feel financially stable?

Goals

- What are your organization's long term goals?
- What are your organization's short term goals?
- What are your long term goals for yourself within your organization?
- What are your goals for your position?
- How has your role changed since you have been in it?

VI.   Example of Reflective Assignments

Part I

Write comprehensive list of all the contributions that you have made to our mission. This can be just a bullet listing but must include –as much as you can recall- all activities, big and small. Many of you have presented speakers, shown the documentaries, taken trips, accepted leadership positions within the group, etc. Use your colleagues to help jog your memory and make sure your list is complete.

Part II

Describe and reflect on how your experience as a Periclean Scholar has had an impact on your (1) family, (2) friends, (3) peers and (4) professors. Make sure that you include your impact on the various (5) community groups (Rotary Clubs, churches, former high schools, etc.) that you may have spoken to and/or gotten donations from. What have you taught them about Namibia and HIV/AIDS? How have they changed their behavior and/or views because of your influence? What have they said to you that make you know you have had an impact on them? This could turn into a long essay, so make it easier on you by breaking it down into sub-sections.

Part III

Revisit your list of accomplishments (Part I) and describe (1) the overall impact these activities had on your undergraduate career, (2) how these activities helped you directly or indirectly in learning and applying the skill sets you learned in your major(s) or minor(s), and (3) enhanced your leadership and organizational skills. In other words, what has it meant to you –both in terms of personal and professional development- to be a member of this program?

Part IV

What advice would you give to the Classes of Periclean Scholars that follow in your footsteps? What mistakes did we make that could or should have been avoided? What successes did we have and how would you advise they learn from these activities? What specific advice would you give to the Mentors of those Classes? To the members of those Classes?

Part V

How do you think your undergraduate career would have unfolded had it not been for this program? And, as a related question, how have your post graduation plans (both short and long term) been impacted by your career as a Periclean Scholar?

Part VI

How do you feel we have done thus far in terms of fulfilling our mission statement? What have we done to educate both the people of the United States and Namibia about the issues surrounding HIV/AIDS? What do you think we can/should do to sustain our impact? What will you do to carry on our mission?

VII. Sample Blog Posts

Class of 2015

The Class of 2015 hosted Christine Buchholz, vice president of Restavek Freedom Foundation at Elon on Tuesday. Buchholz presented to an audience that evening in Moseley. Here's a summary of her presentation.

Imagine living in the year 2014 a second-class citizen in your own home. You are a child, yet you live to serve this family with whom you were sent to live because your biological parents could not afford to support you. You prepare food, which you are not allowed to eat; you help your "siblings" get ready to go to a school where you will never step inside to receive education. You are a child slave in Haiti. You are a restavek.

Vice President of Restavek Freedom Foundation Christine Buchholz imparted this to last night's audience in Moseley 215 during her talk, "Modern Slavery in Haiti: the Restavek Dilemma." The restavek system in Haiti is illegal, but culturally it is widely accepted. It is not uncommon for a rural Haitian woman to give birth to up to 10 children, but because of Haiti's crippling poverty, rural families often can't afford to take care of their children. With hopes of providing them better lives, parents will send their children to another home, typically in an urban area of the country. The connection may be distant, Buchholz explained. Often, restavek children identify their host families as their "godparents," "aunts" or "uncles," though the connection can be more convoluted than that.

Buchholz projected a photo of a group of young smiling Haitian girls. You wouldn't know from their faces in the photograph that they had once been restaveks. Restavek Freedom Foundation established a transitional home for girls taken out of restavek. The home currently holds 12 girls. It is a place of refuge for those who have been abused physically or sexually while in restavek.

At the home, the girls are provided food, shelter, therapy and education. They rebuild their lives in the company of others who become their friends and family. The home, currently located in the

Haitian capital Port-au-Prince, is home for the girls until they are provided a stable situation, whether that is moving back with their biological family, a foster family, higher education, or living on their own if they are old enough.

Through the transitional home, the girls are provided schooling, than vocational training. They make their own jewelry and it is sold, often through events that Restavek Freedom Foundation attends. The girls put the money they make from the jewelry sales into their own bank accounts. Buchholz said some have as much as 1,000 U.S. dollars in their accounts, about $260 more than Haiti's Gross National Income per capita. Buchholz expressed a hope that these girls will go on to start their own businesses or continue their education, but no matter what they end up doing, their future has already taken a turn for the better after having left their previous situations.

A few of the girls, and the transitional home's host mother participate as voices on the radio program Zoukoutap, a drama that follows the stories of multiple characters, one of whom is in restavek. Restavek Freedom teamed up with Population Media Center and recently introduced the program in the hopes of spreading awareness about restavek. Buchholz said that although the restavek system of giving up one's child for a better life is well known and accepted throughout Haiti, rural families are often unaware of the degree of danger their sons or daughters may face when they enter a new home. As plotlines develop and characters grow and change, Restavek Freedom and Population Media Center want to monitor the response of the public in relation to issues such as restavek as they are addressed in the program.

Songs for Freedom, another initiative of Restavek Freedom, has gained enormous attention. The national singing competition began in December 2012. It was designed to spread awareness about restavek through the music and lyrics of young Haitians. 9,000 people attended the finale that year. This year, a contest will be held in every department of Haiti, and the grand finale will be held in Port-au-Prince in August 23rd, 2014.

The result of the competition was more than Buchholz had expected. The lyrics were intense and powerful; the performers acted out the traumatic lives of restaveks. "We tapped into an area of passion for these youths," Buchholz said. The young people were finally given a venue to express their creativity and thoughts. Local media covered the competition; contestants spoke on the radio and television about restavek.

Restavek Freedom Foundation is helping to initiate conversation about the restavek issue. The rest of us should follow suit.

Class of 2016

As the semester comes to a close, the Periclean Scholars Class of 2016 is proud of its accomplishments over the past year. We have formed a partnership with Hope for Honduran Children, and are seriously considering another partnership that may work well with our existing partnerships. We anxiously await the chance to bring these two partners to Elon next fall as Pericleans in Residence with the hopes of determining how our class can be most effective in Honduras.

This past week, we worked together on our two-year-plan. It was exciting to see how far the class has come, as we attempted this overwhelming task in an effective, patient way. Everyone listened to one another and worked off each other's ideas to come up with the most efficient, and feasible, 2-year plan. To tackle this difficult task, we made a chart including a space for each semester starting with the Fall of 2014 and ending with the Spring of 2016. A few major topics that we included in each semester were: fundraising efforts, grant writing and letter writing campaigns, local outreach, and building our partnerships Honduras. We have found that setting specific fundraising goals per-semester is difficult, because we have not committed to a specific project or focus as of now. Instead we decided to set goals of the number of fundraising events we will hold each semester. Looking at the Fall of 2014, the class struggled to determine the best way to keep the Pericleans abroad in contact, and to determine a feasible plan for the fall when the majority of our cohort is studying abroad. We have decided to send one e-mail a week to the students who are abroad, which will include anything we have discussed, and will provide them with the chances to vote when necessary. It was encouraging to see that most of the members who plan to study abroad trust the class to make decisions that will be great for the whole class, and for our partners. Overall we had a very successful discussion as we planned out the rest of our time together, including what we can do Pan-Periclean.

At the end of class, we broke into our committees to give some final updates. We are excited to announce that we have established a pen-pal system with boys living in two different communities in Honduras: the Flor Azul Boys Community and the Transition Home. We have connected with these communities through our partner, Hope for Honduran Children, and are excited to get to know the boys on a more personal level, so that we can really learn from them. Our final group meeting will be this Tuesday, May 13, as we say goodbye to our Pericleans studying abroad, and look forward to the exciting progress we can make next year.

Class of 2017

This week was a combination of classmate presentations and listening to a guest speaker. Overall it was a pretty good example of the various things that we are trying to combine, a basic understanding of the different components of Namibia both contemporarily and historically, as well as forming a solid group dynamic with which we can be both effective and efficient.

On Monday two committees presented: Public Health, and Agriculture, Environment, and Geography. The Public Health group's presentation started with the hot topic of Ebola and the preventative methods that the government and health officials are taking. Moving throughout the presentation topics discussed included prevalent diseases, malnutrition, sanitation, access to clean water, maternal and infant mortality, HIV/Aids, mental health, and challenges with access to care to infrastructure. The Agriculture, Environment, and Geography group also presented on a wide variety of issues in Namibia. The presentation started with geography, giving the class an idea of the various deserts, regions, and national parks. Next came a brief description of the climate with which came a discussion on the rain and dry seasons and the impact that drought can have on farming and community health. Part of the obstacle that is rainfall led the group to explain the effects of climate change on agricultural yields.

The Agriculture, Environment, and Geography ended with the important topic of wildlife conservation.

By gaining a basic understanding of public health, agriculture, environment, and geography our class will be able to begin generating focus or project ideas in a more informed way. With those two presentations came the conclusion of our presentations of various aspects of Namibia. We look forward to possibly forming new committees to move forward with.

Today, our steering committee started class off with a presentation on what they think our next steps should be. They brought up the idea of having seven different committees, which are as follows: committees on committees, fundraising/grants, alumni relations, media/communications, steering, events, and executive. The executive committee would be a group of the "leaders" of each of the other six committees with our Mentor as the head of the executive committee. The steering committee had also talked to one of the 2016s that responded with some positive feedback with what has worked for them. He suggested a vibe watcher (making sure no one gets too heated), a facilitator, an agenda setter, and a secretary. To conclude their presentation, they gave us a handout and we decided as a class that we would use this committee system as base and further discuss the changes needed in the system.

On Monday, at the very end of class, Carol had us take a personality test from the MyPlan website. Rhonda Kosusko came in today to help us understand our results. She explained what each letter meant and gave us countless handouts about each type of personality. She then divided us into groups of four or five, and had us discuss what we thought was important for people to bring to a group. From the activity, we were able to learn the people value different things, and we all need to be respectful to that. At the end of the class period, Carol had us divide into two groups; one group was the extroverts, and one was the introverts, and then continued to divide with the last three categories. We soon learned that everyone is different, and we can use these differences to our advantage. All in all, the week was successful because we learned more about Namibia, and we learned more about each other.

Steering Committee

Steering Committee Meeting Notes (3/12/15)

Reports from classes

- 15's
  - Monthly munchies: March 18th 8-11
  - Fundraiser with Pelicans (need a place)
  - 5K plans being discussed
  - Graduation Stoles: still in the works
  - Class sustainability: creating a club at Elon
  - Partner was featured in documentary; Library is ordering this and maybe we can share this to campus
- 16's
  - Grant writing class next Tuesday
  - Cookies to go-go April 8th
  - Good vibes from partners
  - LUPE meeting went well
  - English lessons continue
- 17's
  - Accountability representatives
  - Mission Statement and email template revisions
  - New contacts: Leonard Shikololo in the north of Namibia

Pan-Periclean Updates

- Handbook -- physical copy by induction (1st draft) but updated every year
- Induction: Periclean of the year (will be announced at induction) Let Arcaro know as soon as it is decided.

Director Updates

- Chiapas
  - Can't send anyone down without fac/staff leadership
  - Need a way to decide who goes on the trip if it happens. We need a faculty/staff person to go
- Search

- o Susie and Kelsey on search committee for assistant director
  - o Ad goes out next Monday -- will proceed from there
- Periclean Foundation
  - o Successor of Periclean alumni foundation (2012)
- 12's Franklin Project Initiative -- pathways of service for year after graduation
  - o Have a Elon fellow for your class to continue your project?

Random Notes:

- Make sure to post your notes on the blog after each class meeting
- Make sure to categorize your notes and use headings and pictures!
- COR 455: Start now to construct; needs to have deliverables
- money for stoles comes from pan-Periclean; think ahead for this
- Steering committee blog post in Periclean Book
- Buttons at induction (perhaps "Peace, Love, Periclean" if we're lucky)!!!

VIII.   Testimonies from Past Periclean Scholars

"Without the Periclean Scholars program, I wouldn't know to ask, "What does this job mean to the world?" Slowly, without me realizing it, the Periclean Scholars program fundamentally shifted my thought process when it came to planning about a career path. The program made me see that the work you do can impact the world, and that you need to find a place that allows you to make an impact."
            -Julie Bourbeau, '06

"Periclean Scholars allowed me to see the similarities we have with our neighbors across the world: the desire to be heard valued and loved."
            -Laura Sinden, '08

"[Periclean Scholars] has taught me about the real places, the real problems, and most importantly, the real people. Periclean Scholars has changed my life."
            -Damon Duncan, '06

"The experiences that I have gained from being a part of Periclean Scholars continue to shape my views on life and the global mindset that I received continues to be a base for me to center myself and keep life in perspective."
            -Emily Sargent, '07

"Periclean scholars has given me a flexible worldview that enables me to see beyond my own privilege and empathically understand the world of poverty, poor health, and inequality. That worldview is the reason I write this message from my desk at a community mental health center where I act as a therapist for marginalized people: people who are often living on the streets and have fallen through the cracks because they do not have insurance or Medicaid."
            -Marissa Morris-Jones, '06

IX.   Further Readings

Abu-Sada, Caroline (ed.). *In the Eyes of Others: How People in Crisis Perceive Humanitarian Aid,* Doctors Without Borders, 2012.

Barnett, Michael. *The Empire of Humanity: A History of Humanitarianism*, Cornell University, 2011.

Bortolotti, Dan. *Hope in Hell: Inside the World of Doctors Without Borders*, Firefly Books, 2010.

Burnett, John. *Where Soldiers Fear to Tread: A Relief Worker's Tale of Survival*, New York: Bantam Books, 2005.

Cain, Ken, Postlewait, Heidi and Thomson, Andrew. *Emergency Sex (And Other Desperate Measures)*, Miramax Books, 2004.

Corbett, Steve and Fikkert, Brian. *When Helping Hurts: How to Alleviate Poverty Without Hurting the Poor and Yourself*, Moody Publishers, 2009.

Coyne, Christopher. *Doing Bad By Doing Good: Why Humanitarian Action Fails*, Stanford University Press, 2013.

Dawes, James. *That the World May Know: Bearing Witness to Atrocity*. Harvard University Press, 2007.

Easterly, William. *The White Man's Burden: Why the West's Efforts to Aid the Rest Have Done So Much Ill and So Little Good*, Penguin Press, 2006.

Easterly, William. *The Tyranny of Experts: Economists, Dictators, and the Forgotten Rights of the Poor* Penguin Press, 2014.

Farah, Nuruddin. *Gifts*, Penguin, 1999.

Farmer, Paul. *Pathologies of Power: Health, Human Rights, and the New War on the Poor*, University of California Press, 2003.

Farmer, Paul. *Haiti after the earthquake*, New York: Public Affairs, 2011.

Greitens, Eric. *The Heart and the Fist: The Education of a Humanitarian and the Making of a Navy Seal*, Mariner Books, 2011.

Hochschild, Adam. *King Leopold's Ghost: The Story of Greed, Terror, and Heroism in Colonial Africa*, Mariner Books, 1999.

Katz, Johnathan. *The Big Red Truck Went By: How the World Cane to Save Haiti and Left Behind a Disaster*, Palgrave, 2013.

Lupton, Robert. *Toxic Charity: How Churches and Charities Hurt Those They Help*, HarperOne (Harper-Collins Publishers), 2011.

Magone, Claire, Neuman, Michael, Weissman, Fabrice (eds.) *Humanitarian Negotiations Revealed: The MSF Experience*, Columbia University Press, 2011.

Mamdani, Mahmood. *Saviors and Survivors: Darfur, Politics, and the War on Terror, Doubleday*, 2009.

Moyo, Dambisa. *Dead Aid: Why Aid is Not Working and How There is a Better Way for Africa*, New York: Farrar, Straus and Giroux, 2009.

Orbinski, James. *An Imperfect Offering: Humanitarian Action for the Twenty-First Century*, Walker & Company, 2008.

Polman, Linda. *War Games (Crisis Caravan): The Story of Aid and War in Modern Times*, Penguin Books, 2010.

Reiff, David. *A Bed For the Night: Humanitarianism in Crisis*, Simon & Shuster, 2002.

Sachs, Jeffery. *The End of Poverty: Economic Possibilities for Our Time*, Penguin Press, 205.

Singer, Peter. *The Life You Can Save: Acting Now to End World Poverty*, Random House, 2009.

Stearns, Jason. *Dancing in the Glory of Monsters: The Collapse of the Congo and the Great War of Africa*, Public Affairs, 2011.

Temple-Raston. *Justice on the Grass: Three Rwandan Journalists, Their Trial for War Crimes, and a Nation's Quest for Redemption*, New York: Free Press, 2005

Wright, Jeff (J). *Missionary, Mercenary, Mystic, Misfit,* Evil Genius Publishing, LLC, 2013.

Wright, Jeff (J). *Disastrous Passion: A Humanitarian Romance Novel,* Evil Genius Publishing, LLC, 2013.

Wright, Jeff(J). *Honor Among Thieves*, Evil Genius Publishing, LLC, (forthconing)2014.

Wright, Jeff (J). *Letters Left Unsent,* Evil Genius Publishing, LLC, 2014.

Mapping Our Success

Edition I – April, 2015
- Editors: Kelsey Lane, Samantha Lubliner, Erin Luther

About The Editors

With the understanding that this book was a well-needed asset for the Periclean Scholars Program at Elon University, students Kelsey Lane, Samantha Lubliner and Erin Luther began the process of compiling "Mapping Our Success". Kelsey and Samantha are both part of the Class of 2017 and Erin is part of the Class of 2016. With the help of Catherine Parsons, the Assistant Program Coordinator, the handbook came to fruition after dedicated hours of editing and compilation. They are all excited to have been a part of creating the first edition of "Mapping Our Success" and look forward to sharing their knowledge of the process with Periclean Scholars in the years to come that will take over editing for future editions.

Made in the USA
Middletown, DE
21 April 2015